Mentoring the Jesus Way

Robert Mounce

To four very special men who, along with their wives, have become exceptionally close to me in the Lord. They are friends since:

Tim and Karen Jobe 1967

Thomas and Laurie Weakley 1975

Gary and Julie Pierce 1996

Ray and Esther Rimbey 2003

Table of Contents

]

]

One

Are important issues simple or complex?

Have you ever wondered how Jesus would go about teaching were he brought into in our contemporary culture? At first, the idea of a first century itinerant preacher in an Ivy League classroom boggles the mind. Yet, at twelve years of age, he did go to the sacred halls of academia of his day where he engaged the religious leaders in serious discussion. Luke 2:47 reports that "all who heard him were astonished at his understanding and the skill with which he answered their questions." I suspect that he could handle a Harvard or Yale exposure as well. However, Jesus' teaching ministry was not with the intelligentsia of his day, but with the common people, those who would leave their workbench and go out to some open area where they could hear his words of instruction. To teach these people, Jesus used parables, short allegorical stories that illustrated a religious or moral truth.

And that is exactly how we learn today. We come to understand what we don't know as it is illustrated by something we do know. We tell a growing child that the world is like a big rubber ball, that is, it is round. Jesus taught the kingdom of God by comparing it to seed planted in various kinds of soil: the richer the soil the more bountiful the growth. He described his teaching method in Mark 4:2, "I taught them many spiritual truths using simple stories from everyday life."

Most people tend to think that the great truths of life are necessarily complex, that science operates in a world of extreme complexity. And it does, but that complexity is essentially connected with what we don't as yet know or what we are in the process of learning, not with the outcome of the scientific activity. Gravity is a very easy scientific axiom to understand in its practical application, but whether it is best described by Einstein's general theory of relativity or by Newton's law of universal gravitation is still a question.

The truths that Jesus taught were those that genuinely matter, not only for today, but for eternity. I don't mean at all to downgrade the advances that are being made in areas such as pharmacological research, medicine, robotics, etc., but I am reminded as a believing Christian that there is an eternity. Truths that deal with matters of the spirit are ultimately more important than those limited to time. To be consistent we must direct our life by our most basic assumptions and beliefs.

]

So I am glad that Jesus taught "spiritual truths using simple stories from everyday life" – that way I can understand. And what does this have to do with living as Jesus lived? The answer is that as he kept his focus on that which was of eternal significance, so should we.

Two

Living under authority

The first story in the gospels where Jesus is seen taking action is his decision to remain in the temple to discuss theological issues with the rabbis while his family left for home (Luke 2:41-52). The family had gone to Jerusalem to celebrate the Passover. Now they were returning and late in the day his parents noted that Jesus was missing. They returned to Jerusalem to look for him. Three days later they found him in the temple in serious discussion with the religious leaders. Jesus had decided that being in "his Father's house" asking and answering questions of the rabbis was more important than returning with the family. But now he went with his parents and returned to Nazareth where he "continued to live under their authority" (v. 51).

You might ask at this point, "What is it that we could possibly learn about imitating Christ from this early incident?" After all, even as a child he was the incarnate Son of God, and we are miserable sinners at best. I think there are at least a couple of lessons in the story for us today.

]

First, by remaining behind he is saying that the spiritual concerns of life are more important than all its secondary issues. I'm not suggesting that we should view Jesus as a super- spiritual young man with an extraordinary longing to be a religious leader. There is nothing about his life that would suggest that. He was simply a young adult with a deep desire to know more about those issues that were central to life. To be like Jesus in this sense is to make the most of every occasion that offers the chance to learn something of spiritual importance.

A second observation is that this experience, which for the moment placed him at the center of attention, did not go to his head. It did not change his responsibility to "live under their [his parents] authority" (v. 51). The normal reaction of youth would be to make the most of the privilege at the expense of any connected responsibility. It could be argued that a boy whose insight into matters spiritual was that he should be free from normal childhood obligations. The mature Christian recognizes that being a child of God does not relieve us from the normal restrictions of life. It is true that we are citizens of another country (the Jerusalem above), but for the time being we live under the authority of the land we used to call home.

So, to live like Jesus is to stay centered on that which is of eternal significance, and to live under the normal restrictions of life.

Three

What would it be like to live like Jesus?

One of the observations about the boy Jesus that I have always liked is Luke's statement that "Jesus grew in both wisdom and stature, gaining the approval of God and all the people" (Luke 2:52). He had astounded the rabbis in Jerusalem with the depth of his understanding and the skill with which he asked and answered questions (v. 47). Now he was back home in Nazareth, a simple hillside town. For a twelve year old boy, that remarkable three day event in Jerusalem was sure a lot to brag about, but Jesus continued his normal life, growing up physically, learning new things day by day, pleasing God, and developing a good reputation with the towns-people.

The essential question we are asking is, "What is it like to live like Jesus?" and this incident gives us a good clue. It suggests that as Jesus was comfortable, both in his hometown and the capital city, we need to embrace the immediate setting in which God has placed us. We may feel that we were meant for better things. The dusty hills of our Nazareth may not seem to be the best in which to share our gifts with the world. That, of course, is our natural response, but

God has placed us exactly where we are at this specific time for his purposes, not ours. Someone said, "To be satisfied with one's lot is to acknowledge that God's plan is better than ours." So the first lesson in living a Christ-like life is accept that we are where we are not because that is what we might want, but because that is how God has planned it.

A second observation is that Jesus was in a process that involved change; the text says "he grew in wisdom." We can understand how he would grow physically, but what about growing in wisdom? Obviously he would grow in knowledge, but "wisdom," (the wise application of knowledge to life) is something quite different. Perhaps that is the very reason why Jesus gained the approval of the towns-people. Nothing is quite so socially positive as mature individuals applying to life all that they have learned about what serves the common good.

The other thing mentioned in the text is that in addition to gaining the approval of people he also gained "the approval of God." This sounds at first as though earlier on he didn't have it, but that would be word play. Every virtue can grow. To love more doesn't imply a former lack of love. What Luke is saying is that as Jesus grew into manhood his life was pleasing to his Father all along the way.

]

So what does the early Jerusalem story tell us about how we are to live as followers of Christ? Very simply, we are to accept and be comfortable wherever God has placed us, we are to grow in our ability to apply the truth we learn to the life we live, and we are to live so as to bring pleasure to God.

Four

The role of Scripture in temptation

After Jesus was baptized, he was led by the Spirit into the desert where he began a lengthy period of fasting (Matt. 4:1-11). After forty days, in which he became absolutely famished, the devil showed up and suggested ways in which he could satisfy that hunger. To the possibility of turning stones into bread, Jesus responded, "Scripture says" and then explained that man needs more than bread to live. The devil's second temptation was for Jesus to throw himself from the top of the temple and allow the angels to protect him. Once again Jesus said, "But scripture also says" and explained that God should not be put on trial. Then the devil offered Jesus complete control over the kingdoms of this world if he would just bow down and worship him. Jesus demanded that Satan leave because "the scriptures say" that only God is to be worshipped. The obvious lesson for us is that God has spoken in scripture and that as we face the temptations of life we are to apply what he has already revealed in them to be his will.

One of the great contributions of the Christian organization, The Navigators, is their emphasis on memorizing scripture. Thousands of young people

]

have gone through their program leading to the mastery of the essential truths in the bible. What is stressed is that when a temptation arises it should immediately be countered by a verse from scripture. On each of the three occasions Jesus responded to the devil's insidious suggestion with an answer from scripture. I find it interesting that God has not left us on our own to figure out how best to live the Christian life, but has revealed his will for every situation. It's all written down. I know of no problem facing the believer that is not answered in the bible.

Cultures differ, but principles are trans-cultural. For example, we know that when Paul says women are to remain quiet in church (1 Tim 2:12) he is not stating some sort of timeless requirement, but pointing out what would be best for a well ordered church in a first century culture in which women were neither educationally or socially equipped for leadership. What scripture teaches is the truth that lies behind its particular cultural expression.

To know what the bible has to say about all the essential aspects of the Christian life is to be prepared with an answer for every trial we may face. To take this responsibility more seriously would enable us to reflect in an ever- increasing way how Jesus dealt with trials.

Five

What was Jesus really like?

On the day he had baptized Jesus, John the Baptist saw him walking by and declared, "There is the Lamb of God!" (John 1:35-51). John's followers went to Jesus and asked where he was staying, to which Jesus responded, "Come along and you will see." One of the major characteristics we see in Jesus is his openness and availability. Not only did the men go with him, but they spent the rest of the day enjoying his presence. Jesus was very open and approachable, one with whom others enjoyed spending time. He was a genuinely hospitable man. One of the men in this group was Andrew.

The first thing he did was to find his brother, Simon, and tell him that they had found the Messiah. The two of them went immediately to see Jesus. When they arrived, Jesus gave Simon the name Cephas, which means, "Rock." The point is that Jesus saw Peter in terms of what he would become. From subsequent accounts we know that Peter was given to quick responses that revealed considerable instability. But Jesus knew what Peter was capable of becoming and dealt with him in that positive way. Jesus was optimistic about the possibility of change.

]

On the following day Jesus decided to go to Galilee, so turning to Philip, he queried, "Would you like to come along with me?" No reason to make the journey by oneself. It is clear that Jesus was very relational. He enjoyed being with his disciples not only to share what he had to teach, but also to enjoy the simple pleasure of getting to know them.

When Nathaniel learned that Jesus was the man about whom Moses had written and that he had come from the town of Nazareth, his response was, "Can anything good come from that place?" When Jesus saw this somewhat pessimistic Nathaniel approaching, he said, "Here comes a true Israelite, a man in whom there is no deceit." Nathaniel may have questioned if anything of worth could possibly come from the little town of Nazareth, but Jesus saw in him the model of a true Israelite – one in whom there is no duplicity. Jesus was insightful. And as the story continues we hear him telling the new convert that he would "see even greater things" than Jesus' immediate recognition of Nathaniel's basic character trait – that is, he would see "heaven standing wide open with the angels of God descending." In addition to insight, Jesus had a profound ability to encourage others.

In these five incidents we learn some important things about Jesus. His encounter with Andrew and his brother Peter shows how approachable and hospitable he was. Viewing Peter in terms of who he would become is both positive and helpful. His desire that Philip go with him to Galilee reveals how comfortable he was in the presence of others. And finally, from the relationship with Nathaniel we see how insightful and encouraging he was. For us to live like Christ is to mirror these same qualities in the world in which we find ourselves. We are to be approachable, positive, relational, insightful, and encouraging.

Six

Should we be performing miracles today?

In the early days of his public ministry Jesus and his mother Mary were invited to a wedding in the Galilean town of Cana. Such weddings often lasted a full week, so at one point, Mary came to her son with the news that they had run out of wine. Jesus told his mother that he didn't share her concern because his time (apparently, his time to reveal that he was the Messiah) had not yet come. However, Jesus told the servants to fill some stone water jars and when they dipped some out it had turned to wine, in fact a wine that was superior to what they had been drinking. The gospel of John points out that this was the first of Jesus' miraculous signs (2:1-11).

The question I want to ask is whether we can be like Jesus when it comes to miracles? Granted, the early church was able to perform acts of healing, but for the most part that gift is not frequently exercised in the contemporary church. Should it be is the question.

It will be well at this point to define "miracle." The British Dictionary says a miracle is "an event that is contrary to the established laws of nature and attributed to a supernatural cause." Other dictionaries say roughly the same in more erudite language. The one thing that is clear is that miracles call for a force outside the human realm and that implies that they are not something we could do by our own power. They are acts of God.

So when the early church was "filled with awe at the many wonders and signs performed by the apostles" (Acts 2:43) it was actually God at work through them. When we say that an apostle performed a miracle what we mean is that God used the apostle as the agent through whom he carried out his supernatural act. All the miracles performed by members of the primitive church were divine acts wrought through humans. They healed the sick and drove out demons, which not only served the physical needs of the afflicted, but helped authenticate the message they delivered. (Acts 8:6 reports that the people paid attention to Philip's message "when they heard and saw the signs which he did.")

Against this background I would suggest that miracles are happening all the time in the contemporary church. Perhaps not the more typical miracles of New Testament days such as healing the sick, but if a miracle is an act of God performed through one of his own, then every answered prayer is a miracle, every intervention of God into the human sphere at our request. Recently a friend involved in

]

campus ministry told me of a number of freshmen who opened their hearts to Christ and were granted forgiveness and eternal life. Was that not a miracle? It was beyond human competence and required the supernatural. Wherever God is at work in this world miracles are happening on a continuing basis. And we can be part of that! We can live like Jesus.

Seven

Can material create non-material?

Almost every person is aware that the material world in which we live (and of which we are a part) is not the only world. This very awareness is part of that other world, a world without boundaries, one in which we are not limited by time or by space. "But," you say, "That is merely our mind at work, our imagination."

But wouldn't that mean that the material (brain) is creating the non- material (imagination)? That seems a bit difficult for me. If there are two realms, then would it not be more reasonable for the non-material to be responsible for the material? After all, it's the sphere you hold to be unlimited. I wouldn't suggest that something like that is what Jesus had in mind when he was talking with Nicodemus (the Jewish scholar) about spiritual birth, but it does open the door to consider a sphere of being that is not material. That Jesus could perform miraculous signs led Nicodemus to acknowledge that God was somehow involved. But the question of being born again in order to enter the kingdom of God left him confused.

So Jesus said, "I tell you the truth, a person cannot enter the kingdom of God unless he is born of water and the Spirit. Physical birth results in a physical

]

being; spiritual birth, in a spiritual being" (John 3:5-6).

I know that the expression "to be born again" has been used in connection with everything from used car sales to a new plan for vacationing, but Jesus was not speaking metaphorically. He was distinguishing between two realities, physical life as we know it and a new kind of life, spiritual. The first brings a child into our world and the second into the world best described as spiritual. Interestingly enough, as in physical life, so also in spiritual life – a person can't experience the realm prior to being born into it. I encourage you to think about it because in both cases confirmation follows birth.

Eight

Who takes the initiative in outreach?

The route to Galilee took Jesus through Samaria, an area considered ceremonially unclean by the Jews. Stopping to rest at the town of Sychar, he sat down by a well while his disciples left to buy something to eat. Just then a Samaritan woman came to draw water and Jesus asked her for a drink. Taken aback, she asked how it could be that he, a Jew, would ask her, a Samaritan, for a drink of water. (Jews considered Samaritans a heretical branch of Judaism and wanted nothing to do with them since even contact would make them ceremonially unclean.) An extended discussion took place (John 4:4–42) in which Jesus identified himself as the Messiah. At that point the disciples returned and were surprised to find Jesus talking with a woman and, of all things, a Samaritan woman.

What I want to point out is that in the discussion with the Samaritan woman, it was Jesus who took the initiative. What would be expected would be for Jesus to have found someone else to ask the woman on his behalf. But Jesus took the first step; he was the one who broke the silence and asked the woman for help. As you know, we are looking at what Jesus did rather

]

than what he said, and that in order to learn how to live a Christ-like life. What we see here is that Jesus opened the discussion. He didn't wait to be spoken to, but seeing a woman by the well needing a drink of water, he initiated the discussion. This readiness to move things forward continued throughout his ministry. For example, on the evening before his crucifixion he washed his disciples feet and said, "I have set you an example that you should do as I have done for you." (John 13:15)

In today's narrative we see him doing exactly that very thing. Not waiting for the woman to speak to him (and she wouldn't, being both a woman and a Samaritan), Jesus opened the discussion with a simple request. There is no question but that we are to take the initiative whenever the opportunity arises to share the good news about the "water that gives life."

Nine

A busy day for Jesus

It had been a busy day for Jesus. It was the Sabbath and we were in Capernaum so we went to the local synagogue where Jesus was teaching. The religious authorities were amazed at his insight and the skill with which he taught. At one point a man with a demon began to shriek at the top of his lungs and Jesus had to cast the demon out of him. Then after the service we went to Simon's house where we found Simon's mother ill with a fever. Jesus healed her and when people with various diseases heard about it they came from all over town to be healed. It was a long and tiring big day for sure! So the next morning Jesus simply rolled over and told his disciples to let him sleep.

Wait a minute!! That can't be what the Scriptures say! Right. All three synoptic gospels note that while it was still dark, Jesus slipped out of the house and found a lonely place where he could be by himself and pray. Later in the morning the disciples realized he was not around so they set out to find him. When they found him they explained that all sorts of people were looking for him in order to be healed, so it was time for him to go back to work.

]

Jesus' response was that his purpose in coming was to preach the good news and that it was now time for him to leave Capernaum to carry out his mission in Galilee.

Two things strike me about Jesus in this encounter, and both provide guidance on how to live the Christian life. First, the absolute centrality of prayer. After that extremely exhausting day Jesus demonstrated that his spiritual need for renewal was greater than his physical need for sleep. This strongly implies that our greatest need, as we share with others the message of the cross, is the absolute centrality of prayer. Spiritual battles are won by dependence on God, not by having on hand the latest apologetic weapon available. The enemy is far less concerned with all the time we spend mapping out a program for evangelism than they are with our decision to drop to our knees and pray that his will be done.

The second point is that nothing distracted Jesus from this core purpose in life. He said, "I must preach the good news about my Father's kingdom. That's why I came out here this morning; I needed to be with the Father." He maintained his priorities. And the lesson for us is clear: As Christians, we must keep our lives in focus. I encourage you to take a break and think again on what is central for you. What has God assigned for you to do? How can you best carry it out? Not suggesting that you have to essentially "quit living" (e.g., no time with the family, no vacations, little sleep), but that you keep in mind that while all these other things are important they should not become our purpose in life. Let them serve to help us achieve our goal, not become that goal.

Ten

Did Jesus need to pray?

Fairly early in Jesus' ministry he met a leper who longed to be healed. Moved with pity, Jesus healed the man and sent him to a priest who would certify that the cure was effective. The leper, however, couldn't help but rush out and tell everyone what had happened. Even though Jesus was spending most of his time out in the country, people kept coming from everywhere in the region to be healed. At that point Jesus did something that was extremely important. Read Luke 5:12-16 and note the final sentence: "Because of the crowds I frequently withdrew to some deserted place to pray." The point is clear – the absolute necessity of prayer.

Reflect for a moment on the fact that the narrative is describing the ministry of none other than Jesus Christ, the incarnate Son of the eternal God. It is he, not one of us mortals, who felt the need to withdraw for a time from meeting the needs of others. What was more important than anything else at that point was time with his heavenly Father. If Jesus needed spiritual rest and renewal what can be said about us human beings flawed by sin?

Why is it that prayer is so essential for a well-lived Christian life? Scripture teaches that we are engaged in a spiritual battle. In his letter to the Ephesian church, Paul wrote: "Our battle is not against enemies in the physical world, but against the spiritual forces of evil in the heavenly world" (6:12). Would any sane person think even for a moment that we could handle such adversaries with nothing but our native skills? Spiritual battles are won with spiritual weapons and prayer is the one available to us. Prayer elicits the resources of God to withstand and then defeat the wicked powers of evil. If Jesus needed quiet time for prayer what could possibly be said of us?

But prayer is not simply the means of victory in spiritual conflict; it is also the ultimate experience of friendship with a loving Father. He delights in our companionship. He looks forward to those beautiful moments when together we share the joy of oneness. Knowing God fully is the richest of all his blessings and prayer opens that door.

]

Eleven

Who were the outcasts?

One day as Jesus was out walking along the Sea of Galilee he passed by one of the Roman tax houses. Glancing inside, he caught sight of Levi, the Jewish official in charge of collecting taxes for the Romans (not an enviable position for a Jew!). Jesus invited this "outcast" to become one of his followers, so he left everything, business and all, and went with Jesus. Not only that, but he was so excited about this new chapter in his life that he prepared a feast and invited all his friends to come and meet his new acquaintance, Jesus. When the Pharisees and other religious Jews heard about this they were indignant. How could Jesus associate with a tax gatherer and his ceremonially unclean friends? A respectable Jew simply wouldn't take the risk.

Jesus' explanation was that he hadn't come for the benefit of the "virtuous" (self-claimed of course), but for the "sinners" (Mark 2:17). That being the case, he ministered to those who were open to being "healed" – social outcasts, at least that was what the religious Jew thought about them.

So what can we learn from the way Jesus handled this situation? One thing is that he was not hampered in his ministry by the views of the religious hierarchy. He understood that he was called to help those who were open to the truth. Unfortunately, the practice of religion often blinds people as to what their religion professes to teach. The "doing" of it takes the place of what it essentially professes to be. Practice trumps reality. The Jewish Pharisee was committed to the way in which his religion had been practiced over the years, but clueless as to the change it was meant to accomplish in his life.

What about today? For instance, does the average Christian understand the apostle Paul when he says that becoming a follower of Christ involves a death (complete separation) to sin and a resurrection to a new and transformed life in Christ (read Romans 6)? Scripture doesn't support the idea that church attendance guarantees heaven. Those who might think that way would be the "virtuous" in Jesus' statement about those he wouldn't be helping.

Today's "outcasts" are not necessarily those who live on the far edge of morality, but those who are open to hear and respond to the good news that Jesus has a better way. It would appear that those are the ones to whom we also are to direct our ministry. The gospel doesn't beg sinners to change, but offers the answers to life's problems to all who are open to

]

change. Someone said that God is a gentleman who offers help, not a bully who demands change.

Twelve

Can anger be Christ-like?

It was the Sabbath and Jesus was at the synagogue as usual. The religious authorities were watching him closely to see if he would dare, on the Sabbath, to heal a man with a withered hand. If he did, that would allow them to bring a charge against him. So Jesus asked them if one of their animals had fallen into a pit on a Sabbath would they rescue it? Assuming a positive response, Jesus went on to ask why then would it be wrong to heal a man's hand on the Sabbath? Should he leave the man's hand withered? The text says that dead silence filled the room (Mark 3:4). Jesus was "deeply distressed by their indifference to human distress." After looking around the room at each of them in "anger" he restored the hand of the disabled man.

Granted, contemporary Christianity has no restrictions like that although certain branches of the church would rather not have their ritualism questioned. Jesus was deeply concerned with the religious leaders' indifference to human suffering. So the question for us is whether we can or should join him in his opposition to such attitudes. It would seem that the answer should be Yes, but if you actually carried through with it, the local congregation would probably take offense.

The most overused injunction in scripture is, "Thou shall not judge." To call attention to the other person's questionable conduct is often considered the greater offense. It is true that Jesus is Jesus, and we aren't!

He was truly man and it was as a man like us that he reacted as he did. So my answer is that strong opposition to such things as hypocrisy and indifference to evil is a Christ-like attitude. But, let our opposition against the failures of others be an act of love.

Thirteen

Is martyrdom necessary?

In the gospel of Matthew we read the story of Jesus healing a man's withered hand on the Sabbath. When the religious clerics saw this "violation" of the Sabbath they were extremely displeased. Storming out of the synagogue they met with the Herodians on how they could destroy this man. "Aware of their plot to kill him, Jesus withdrew with his disciples to the shores of Lake Galilee" (Mark 3:6-7). A question for those who model life after Jesus is, "If someday my life is actually threatened for what I believe, should I remain true to my convictions or take cover?" On the basis of what Jesus did in this situation it would seem that the martyrs of the early church may have been foolish for having chosen the lions rather than recant.

We know, of course, that Jesus was anything but a coward. When opposed by the clerics in Jerusalem who were in cahoots with Rome he remained true all the way to the cross. We know from scripture that had he needed help his Father could have dispatched "more than twelve legions of angels" for his protection (Matt. 26:53). We can certainly rule out timidity or cowardice as the motivating factor for his retreat to the lake.

We do not know exactly why he withdrew from danger on this occasion, but it would seem that he merely wanted to continue this stage of his ministry and that would have been less likely had he exposed himself needlessly to danger. In time, his adversaries did carry out their villainous plan, but in the meantime the crowds needed to hear the message of the kingdom and the sick needed to be healed. I see Jesus as a thoughtful person who went about his mission in a rather quiet and humble way. Tired from the day's journey he sat by the well and let his disciples go for food (John 4). Even the day before he was crucified, he gathered with the Twelve for a quiet meal. "Let not your heart be troubled" characterized his life. So, here in our verse when he was threatened by angry clerics, Jesus simply decided that it would be better for him to move out of such a menacing environment and go where he would be more free to carry out the father's work.

Fourteen

Why did Jesus have to pray?

Early in his public ministry Jesus came to the point where had to make an important decision. He knew he could not carry out his responsibility to proclaim the kingdom of God all by himself. The task called on him to select others who would work with him. So what did he do? He didn't set up a recruiting center, but rather "went up onto the mountain to spend the night in prayer." Only then could he choose twelve disciples who would (1) be his "closest companions," (2) "learn from him," and (3) "go out and proclaim his message" (*Jesus, In His Own Words*, p. 49). The lesson is obvious: important decisions call for extended time in prayer. Let's think about this together.

It seems to me that everyone knows what prayer is, but no one knows how it works. Whenever there is a national tragedy the news media assures the families of their prayers. And there is probably no person alive today who at some place in their three- score-and-ten haven't lifted their voice in prayer. But what is it? How does it work?

We acknowledge that God is sovereign. He is in control of all he created. But when we pray and God answers our prayer doesn't something happen that would not have happened had we not asked? Then who made it happen? The answer is obvious, but if we made it happen in what sense was the Sovereign God in control? One suggestion is that of his own free will God decided to limit his sovereignty so that only within a narrow range did those he created have the freedom to choose. But what if their decision was for evil to win over good? It gets complicated doesn't it!

I'm quite sure that the power of prayer doesn't depend on our understanding of how it works. Part of living by faith is to follow whatever path it lays out. And this is where we often fall short. Jesus had the task of choosing and preparing twelve men so he turned immediately to prayer. He needed to know the Father's mind on this and that took an all-night session. This provides for us an important lesson on discerning God's will in a given situation. If prayer were simply getting information on the right way to do something that would make it easy. But prayer is also the character creating experience of becoming more like Christ. The decision that needs to be made is only a part of the larger story. In fact, its major role is to provide the opportunity for our own spiritual growth. So the next time you find yourself at the point of "choosing twelve good men," remember that God wants you to spend some extended time with Him for your own growth. The "decision" may be secondary.

Fifteen

Compassion must lead to action

As Jesus and his disciples approached the town of Nain they were met by a funeral procession. It was an especially sad affair because the deceased was the only son of a widow. When Jesus saw the mother, his heart was moved with compassion.

Reaching out, he touched the coffin and the procession came to a stop. Jesus simply said, "Wake up," and the corpse sat up and began to talk. Then Jesus presented the boy to his mother and the crowd could scarcely believe what they were watching. They raised their voices in prayer and news of this event spread like fire throughout the countryside (Luke 7:11-17).

Two things are important: the first is Jesus' compassionate reaction to human sorrow. The mother had lost her husband and this made their son the only family she knew. Now he was gone and she was alone. Jesus saw the sadness in her eyes and was deeply touched by her anguish. This personal concern alone is an example of tender compassion for the heavy of heart, but it didn't stop there; he hadn't yet done all that he could.

Reaching out, Jesus touched the coffin and the

procession came to a halt. Then Jesus told the dead son to rise to life. He did and Jesus presented this "newborn" to his mother. The emotion Jesus displayed was not for the effect it might have on those watching, but was a genuine reaction to her need.

This brings a second observation: genuine compassion led to action. Emotion is not for the benefit of the one responding, but is the inevitable response to need wherever it occurs. One cannot care yet stand idly by in a time of misfortune. If compassion is nothing but an emotion then it has been stripped of its essential meaning.

What if we were part of a funeral procession like this? Would we speak kindly to the sorrowing mother? Would we check to see if her every day needs were being take care of? Would we drop by to spend a bit of time with her? Would we make sure that she knew we would be praying for her in her time of bereavement? If so, then our compassion would be real and we would be doing what our mentor Jesus would.

Sixteen

Jesus, our mentor teaches trust

Earlier that day Jesus had brought back to life the son of the widow of Nain, but now that evening had come he went aboard a boat and headed across the lake with his disciples. Suddenly a fierce storm arose and waves began to crash over the deck. The disciples were terrified. They rushed to Jesus and shrieked for him to save them. But Jesus was comfortably asleep on a cushion in the stern of the boat! Their cries for help woke Jesus who chided them very calmly for their failure to trust and for their being so easily frightened. Then he got up and ordered the wind and the waves to cease, and everything became perfectly calm. The disciples shook their heads in amazement that even the wind and the waves were under his control.

From the standpoint of the disciples, Jesus' reaction to the raging storm and all its commotion was remarkable. He was actually asleep with waves pounding over the rails. When they woke him up he rebuked them for their failure to trust him. One could argue that having seen Jesus perform numerous miracles they would have expected him to be fully able to handle this situation. But there was a lesson to be learned.

In our quest to learn how Jesus reacted to life's many circumstances we ask why he did what he did. Granted it is speculation, but it seems as if he had planned the entire affair. He undoubtedly knew the storm was on its way and he chose to be asleep at the critical moment to heighten their failure. It appears that once again he wanted them to understand that there was nothing in the created world that was outside of his control. And this basic fact is as important for us today as it was for them. We need to live with the assurance that there is nothing outside the control of God. That basic insight should remove all fear from our lives. God is sovereign and he is in control. What we should learn from the way Jesus handled the situation is that we need to be on watch for those opportunities where we, by our confidence in God, can help others to trust that God knows what he is doing. Jesus used the coming storm to teach the disciples how to trust completely in God. We can do the same. The truth is that we are mentoring (in the sense of influencing) others whether we want to or not because they are watching how we weather the storms of life. Let's do it the right way and show by our steadfastness that God knows what he is doing and that there is always something to learn in every passing chapter of life.

Seventeen

Fearless and Composed

The story of the Gadarene demoniac has always struck me as an especially difficult experience in the life of Jesus. Among other things it revealed an unusual willingness to accept rejection by the very ones he had served. On the far side of the Lake in the region of the Gerasenes there lived a man who was possessed by an evil spirit. When I say, "lived," I mean that since he was no longer able to be with others he had gone into the burial caves outside the city. Night and day he wandered among the tombs, stark naked, howling and gnashing himself with sharp stones. The townspeople were frightened to death of this violent demonic and had tried to tie him up in chains, but he was always able to break free. When this demoniac saw Jesus he rushed toward him, fell at his feet and begged not to be tormented ahead of time. On a nearby hillside was a large herd of pigs. At the evil spirits' request Jesus sent them out of the man and into the pigs who immediately rushed down into the lake and destroyed themselves. The man was cured and wanted to stay with Jesus, but the event had caused such a stir among the townspeople that they pled with Jesus to leave, which he did (Mark 5:1- 20).

What do we see in Jesus demeanor and actions that will help us to live today in a similar fashion?

Certainly one thing is his total lack of fear of the man possessed by so many demons that he was called by the name "Legion." When he came running up to Jesus with the evil spirits screaming through him, Jesus calmly asked him his name. Such composure is remarkable.

The other quality I see in Jesus is his ability to accept with composure the rejection of the people from whose community this wretched man had been removed. Instead of joyfully celebrating the new day, they begged Jesus to leave. So, after telling the demoniac to go back to his friends and tell them of the mercy he had received from the Lord, Jesus moved on to whatever would be next. Like a true prophet he spoke the truth of God and allowed the hearers to react as they would.

To live like Jesus is to react as he did regardless of the danger involved. Should we find ourselves in an unstable situation, as Jesus did in today's narrative, we are to face it without fear, in the most effective manner available, and without expectation of appreciation. That's what Jesus did and, since he is our mentor, we now have a model of how we are to live – courageously, and without expectation of approval.

Eighteen

Jesus' Response to Need

In reading the story about the healing of Jairus'
daughter (with the account of the woman suffering
from a hemorrhage included) I was once again
impressed with Jesus' reactions to the various
emergencies he encountered. Join me as we walk
reflectively through the narrative.

Jesus was ministering to an enthusiastic crowd
along the western shore of the Lake when an official in
the local synagogue by the name of Jairus came and
asked him to come and save his young daughter who
was dying. The text reads, "So I rose and left with my
disciples for the house of Jairus." En route a woman
who had suffered for years with constant bleeding
slipped up behind Jesus and touched one of the
tassels on his cloak. Once again Jesus stopped, turned
to the crowd and asked, "Who touched me?" The
disciples thought that would be impossible because
people were crowding so close around him. But Jesus
"kept trying to locate the person" because he had felt
"healing power go out." The woman fell at his feet
and was sent away healed.

Arriving at the house of Jairus, Jesus was met by
professional mourners who made fun of him when he

told them the girl was merely sleeping. They knew, of course, that she had died. Jesus and the girl's parents went to where the girl was lying and Jesus "took the girl by the hand." She stood to her feet and began to walk around. Then Jesus "instructed the parents to give her something to eat."

I have emphasized those statements that reveal what Jesus did at a number of stages along the way. So let's review them. When Jairus appeared asking for help we read, "So I rose and left." No hesitation. Whenever a need arose Jesus took action. It was the thing to do. When the woman with the flow of blood simply touched his cloak he stopped and asked, "Who touched me?" When he "felt healing power go out" he stopped to encourage that person and commend her for her faith. He was not deterred by the snide comments and laughter of the mourners, but went to the little girl's side and said, "*Tabitha cumi,*" which is Aramaic for, "Little girl, I say to you, arise." Then, lest in their joy they might forget their daughter's immediate need for food he reminded the parents.

What emerges from this double narrative is the picture of a loving caregiver who responded without hesitation to the needs of others whatever they might be. Distance did not deter him, nor did the failure of his disciples to grasp the significance of the touch of a single needy person, nor did the amusement of the funeral professionals. He carried through with his responsibility to restore to health a little girl.

And how are we to live like this? Frankly I'm not sure, but one way to begin is to ask our mentor, Jesus, to make us more aware of specific needs and give us the determination to live as he did.

Nineteen

The compassionate Jesus

Jesus continued to proclaim the good news as he made his way through the towns and villages of Galilee. Wherever he went there were people who needed his healing touch. Matthew records that those who crowded around him were "confused and helpless, like sheep without a shepherd" (9:35). So how did their distress affect Jesus emotionally and what did he do about it? We know that he told them that God's kingdom was being established on earth and that they should repent (Matt. 3:2; 4:17), but what was his instinctual reaction to them in their need? Matthew writes that Jesus' heart was "filled with compassion" (9:36).

The Greek word for compassion refers to one's visceral area. To be "filled with compassion" means to feel in one's body what might be called an emotional equivalent to what another person is experiencing. It is deep bonding with another. Compassion carries its own price; it costs to care. One might ask of what importance is it that we experience such a reaction when we find ourselves with others in need? The answer is simple; apart from compassion we are far less apt to do something about it.

God has made us as we are and given us the capacity to care about the distress of a fellow human being. We are God's creatures and intended to love and be of help to one another. Had sin not entered the world it would have been our natural reaction to the pain or anguish of another. As the sinless Son of God, Jesus shows us what life beyond the pervasive influence of sin is like. When we see another in distress we are moved with compassion. It's what God intended for human relationships, but it has been thrown off track by the dominance of sin in our world.

Compassion is a strong and compelling word. We know it in a limited sense, but I expect that in the relationships of eternity, while there will be no suffering or tears, should there be, we would immediately be moved with compassion. Among certain groups, a show of compassion is considered a sign of weakness. Certainly it is not masculine, they say. To the contrary, compassion is so strong that there is nothing that can ever keep it from expressing itself openly without regard for public reaction. The Dalai Lama is right on target when he says that "love and compassion are not luxuries, but necessities, and without them humanity cannot survive."

Twenty

How to do the undoable

The time had come for Jesus to expand his ministry. For that he needed the help of others, so he selected twelve men as his spokesmen and sent them out to the "lost sheep of the house is Israel." These twelve were assigned the responsibility of announcing that the kingdom of heaven was at hand – but that was not all. They were also to heal the sick, bring the dead back to life, cleanse the lepers, and cast out demons (Matt. 10:8). It seems that the spreading-the-kingdom-message part could be done fairly easily, but the healing, bringing people back to life, and casting out demons was another story! That's quite a different task. For this they would need some power outside of themselves, a supernatural enablement. Such things simply do not happen in what we call normal life.

Of course Jesus knew this, so as the text says, he "selected twelve disciples and gave them the authority to cast out demons and cure diseases and illnesses of every kind" (Matt. 10:1 and following).

The Greek word for authority means "the right to control" which in turn implies the power necessary to accomplish the task. Scripture teaches that God is the ultimate source of all authority. He is the potter who, from a shapeless lump of clay, can fashion anything he likes (Rom 9:21). He has granted this same authority to Jesus. Matthew writes that the resurrected Christ has been given all authority in heaven and on earth (28:18). Jesus, in turn, grants to his disciples the authority to heal and cast out demons. They are to fulfill their mission not in their own strength, but by the supernatural power given to them by God to accomplish that which otherwise would be impossible.

The question I raise is, to what extent has God given this sort of authority to the church in our day? Can we carry out our responsibilities using natural gifts, or is something supernatural required? When we are sent to console a grieving mother who has lost a young child can we do anything in our own strength or is each occasion an opportunity to minister grace and help that depends absolutely upon the supernatural presence of God? I believe it is the latter. God is still active in and through his "staff" of believing Christians to heal the full range of spiritual ills that plague the ever-expanding body of Christ. To put it succinctly, God still selects his "twelve" and empowers us to do his will. His compassion is expressed through his emissaries. His redeeming love is announced through his prophets. He grants to us sinners, transformed by his redemptive love, the authority to do what he wants done. We are those empowered by God to "heal" in every sort of way. It's all part of living a Christ- like life.

Twenty-one

How to make truth personal

When John the Baptist heard about this Jewish man, Jesus, what he was teaching and how he was healing people with all sorts of diseases, he questioned to himself whether or not this could be the man that he had been declaring would come in fulfillment of Messianic prophecy. So he sent two of his followers to find out. They asked Jesus the question and got a less than definitive answer; at best it was not a clear cut Yes or No. Jesus sent the men back to John the Baptist, not with an answer, but with a recommendation that they tell him what they had seen and heard – that is, that "the blind are made to see, the lame start to walk, lepers are being cleansed, the deaf can hear, the dead are raised up, and the poor have the good news proclaimed to them" (Matt. 11:12). I am sure the messengers expected a much simpler answer.

Why did Jesus respond as he did? My answer would be – and it's implied rather than stated – that he wanted John to think it all through and come to a more complete understanding himself. He wanted him to reflect on the remarkable things that were happening in the land and to understand the fuller meaning of the long-awaited coming of the Messiah. Truth is more powerful when it comes as a result of one's own thought process than if someone tells it to you. I believe Jesus wanted John to reflect on the marvelous things that were happening and come to a personal conclusion. Jesus was the coming one he had been announcing.

The broader implication is that Jesus would have us reflect seriously on the deeper issues of life. I'm not talking about getting involved in groups for semi-intellectual discussions, but rather giving careful and private consideration to the more central issues of life. We need to think long and hard about what God is teaching us through scripture – about such things as life itself, the fact that for the believer, life is eternal, the vital importance of personal relationships, and many more. It is in private moments like this that we begin to understand with all humility what God has to say about those issues that are truly significant. Truth needs to become our truth in the sense that we not only understand it, but that we express it in the way we live out our seventy plus years.

I believe that God takes great delight in personally guiding us through the process of learning in this more complete sense. Truth is not an abstract concept, but a guide for life – it is meant to be lived.

God the Father, with the able assistance of God the Holy Spirit, is a mentor who genuinely cares that we understand in depth how to live a Christ-like life.

Twenty-Two

Rebuke sin, do it in love

This next action of Jesus may be a bit shocking to those who have always thought of Jesus as the "gentle Nazarene." For quite some time he had been going from town to town teaching and performing all sorts of miracles. But Matthew tells us that in time Jesus "began to openly criticize the cities in which he had done most of his miracles" (Matt. 1:20). The Greek verb is *oneidizo*, which means (1) to find fault in a way that demeans the other, or (2) to find justifiable fault with someone (Bauer places our verse in the second category).

The NIV has "denounce," the NET has "criticize," and others translate "reproach." Matthew goes on to explain that Jesus was criticizing them "because they didn't repent of their sins." They should have listened to his message, been convinced by his power to do miracles, and repented of their sins – but they didn't. The following verses describe the seriousness of their failure – the fate of Capernaum is "to be thrown down to Hades, the place of the dead" and even the wicked city of Sodom is to be judged less severely. So no matter how you look at it, Jesus was critical of those who did not repent.

Now the question for us is: Do we have a responsibility to act in a similar way? Is it Christ-like to pronounce the doom that is about to fall on those who have had every chance to repent, but refused to do so? Or is this the prerogative of Jesus the Son of God alone? But wait, didn't we start with the premise that Jesus lived out his life as one of us, not dipping into his divinity for power unavailable to us? If he resorted to his power as the eternal Son to perform miracles, then of course we cannot be expected to live like Christ in those areas. But we have taken the other position. He lived among us as one of us, drawing upon the Spirit in the same way that we can.

That we can proclaim the truth of the scripture is perfectly clear. In fact, we are called to do that. That we can declare the tragic results of disbelief is clear. However, we also know that we are to do it in love. Jesus certainly loved the people he came to die for, even those he is speaking to in such a severe manner. His way to express love in the passage under consideration may seem strange to us, but we can leave that with him. What we do know is that when we meet resistance to the good news we are sharing, we are to do it in love. I believe our conscience will be a good guide at this point. Correct sinfulness where appropriate, but do it in a way consistent with love.

Twenty-three
Child-like in prayer

The prayer that begins, "Our Father, who art in heaven" is normally referred to as the Lord's Prayer, but since his disciples had just asked him to teach them how to pray it should probably be called the Disciples' Prayer. In any case, a bit later on in his Galilean ministry we are privileged to listen to Jesus as he prays. It is recorded in Matthew 11:25: "Inspired with joy by the Holy Spirit, I prayed: "I praise you Father, Lord of heaven and earth, that although you have hidden these truths from the wise and discerning, you have made them known to the childlike." So much can be learned if we allow him to be our mentor, as we learn how to pray as he did.

The first thing that strikes me about his prayer is that it was inspired by the Holy Spirit. It was the joy of the Spirit that moved him to pray. So often we think of prayer as a serious obligation to stay in contact with God and bring before him such issues as physical health, how to meet the traumas of life, and thanks that it didn't rain.

By contrast, it was the sheer joy of the Spirit's presence that brought forth praise from the Son of God. How can we not pray if we recognize that the

Holy Spirit is present and wants to talk it all over with us? Remember that the Holy Spirit is one with God the Father and God the Son. Some have referred to him as the "shy member of the trinity" as though he wasn't quite sure of his status and didn't want to draw the spotlight. To genuinely sense the presence and power of the Spirit leads to an incomprehensible joy that must of necessity give birth to prayer.

The other thing that stands out for me is that the eternal truths he was teaching were hidden from "the wise and discerning," but were made known to "the childlike." Why is it that spiritual truth doesn't seem to make sense to the intellectual, but is easily grasped by the innocent? Perhaps because the world's intellectual giants are by definition those who have ventured ahead of us and don't need any insight we might come up with. Ignorance is such a serious fault because it doesn't know that it doesn't know. The child-like can accept spiritual truth because, unlike the phony analyst, it doesn't threaten their certainty that there is nothing they need to learn. The truly wise know how little is known even of our natural world, to say nothing of all that lies in regions beyond.

Jesus, inspired by the joy of the Spirit, lifts his voice in praise, thanking the Father for revealing his truth to the childlike. Three quick suggestions: stay open to the Spirit, be grateful to the Father, and active in praise – as is the Son.

Twenty-four
Letting God be in control

When you read the gospels you come away with the feeling that while "the common people heard him gladly" (as the well-known clause in the King James has it), that wasn't true of the religious hierarchy. What Jesus was doing, as well as what he was teaching, was an affront to their religious system. Since they were normally in control, due to their elevated position in the clerical hierarchy, they were annoyed by the way people were accepting the relatively simple approach of Jesus. It's not amusing to be deprived of the pleasure of exercising power. They wouldn't admit it, but as we know, the possession and exercise of power is the normally unexpressed goal of sinful man at every level.

Let's look at the context in Mark 2 to get the larger picture. One day Jesus and his disciples were walking along beside a wheat field. They were hungry so they picked some grain. The problem was that it was the Sabbath and the Pharisees, who were always on the watch for violations, confronted them for their "unlawful conduct." Jesus responded by pointing out that what they had done was a common practice and that scripture taught that "the Sabbath was made for the sake of man," not the other way around (v. 27). The religious leaders were furious, but Jesus continued day by day to heal all who were ill from various diseases.

When he went into a synagogue the Pharisees were there, waiting to see if he would heal a man with a shriveled hand. Jesus looked at them in anger and told the man to stretch out his hand. Jesus then restored the hand making it better than new. At this point the Pharisees decided to get together with the Herodians (normally they were at odds) to plan some way to get rid of Jesus for good.

At this critical point Jesus decided to withdraw with his disciples to Lake Galilee. Why would he do that? Was he a coward who feared for his life? By no means! Were that true he never would have continued his ministry of healing the sick and casting out demons. No. He withdrew because he knew that his time had not yet come. He understood that his destiny was the cross and that no plan devised by man could alter that.

There is a striking need among God's people to live with that same confidence. The life of every believer is part of a divine plan and what God has willed, will in time come to pass. While we are not pawns, robotically responding to divine directions, at the end of our days we'll realize that He was the one in charge every step along the way. This removes all uncertainty from life. It frees us from the responsibility of being in charge. God is the one in control and he knows the right course of action at every point along the way. How fortunate we are to be able to take our hands off the steering wheel of life and simply enjoy the ride.

Twenty-five

Did Jesus ever get angry?

In an earlier blog I wrote that on one occasion Jesus left Jerusalem for Lake Galilee because his life was being threatened by the religious establishment. In contrast to the clerics who were intent on putting him to death, Jesus appeared to be a calm and gentle man.

However, it also seems that on occasion his anger did rise. In Matthew 12 he severely rebuked the religious leaders who claimed that he had an "unclean" (read "Satanic") spirit. He castigated them saying, "You brood of vipers! How can you say anything good since you are evil" (v. 34)? To call leaders of the religious elite "vipers" would be to reprimand them in the worst possible way. But Jesus was angry. The sacred tradition that he had been taught to honor and respect was being violated by the very ones charged to honor it. In the following verse Jesus says that they are evil and will have to answer for every thoughtless word they have spoken.

Since believers have always been urged to live Christ-like lives, does not Jesus' response on this occasion allow us to become angry? Does it not suggest that where Christian truth is being distorted anger is permissible? That is what Jesus did. The rebuttal that pops to mind is that Jesus also walked on water, so why shouldn't we follow his example at this point? The answer, of course, is that we are not Jesus.

While our lives cannot duplicate his in a precise way, we are to allow his indwelling presence to transform us to be like him. Sanctification (the biblical word for becoming more like Jesus) is a life- long process not an instantaneous reversal of all we are as children of Adam.

Yes, there are times when Christians should be angry. It is clear that God hates sin and so should we. Paul condones Christian anger, but cautions "in your anger do not sin" (Eph. 4:26).

Obviously, since God is who he is, we can't pretend to hate sin exactly as he does. His is a righteous anger while ours at best is an anger that should be expressed with care and only in connection with an acknowledged injustice.

Twenty-six

Jesus as brother

One day when Jesus was teaching, his mother and brothers arrived but were unable to work their way through the crowd to get to him. So they sent a message asking him to come out where they could speak to him (Mark 3:31ff). (Shortly before this they had heard about the large crowds he was attracting so they had tried to bring him home thinking that he was out of his mind; v. 21). Getting the message, Jesus asked rhetorically, "Who is my mother, and who are my brothers?" Then looking around and pointing to his disciples he said, "Look, these are my mother and my brothers" and added that whoever did the will of God was his brother, sister, or mother (v. 35).

The question that arises is Jesus' apparent indifference to his own family. Of all people one would think that Jesus would have been more sensitive to the mother who had nurtured him and the siblings who had grown up at his side. Here, once again, it will be helpful to pay attention to context. Shortly before this episode, Jesus had chosen the Twelve to be with him and become bearers of the message of the coming kingdom. Wherever Jesus went he was surrounded by large crowds.

Using simple stories taken from everyday life he taught them about the ways of God, how to live in a world that had had gone astray. When he wasn't teaching, he was healing. The lame and the blind along with the demon possessed came for his healing touch and went away cured. These highly personal experiences emphasize the oneness that existed in the growing family of God. It was without rebuke that he could look into the face of those who were listening to him and pronounce them family – his mother, his sister, his brothers.

Although we have no way of looking into the mind of Jesus, it is not difficult to imagine how this new family of believers was of increasing importance. In life, a second love in no way disparages the first. That Jesus was a member of this new spiritual family in no way diminished his love for his earthly family. That he was a loving son is clear from his words to his mother from the cross, "Mother dear, John is now your son" and to his beloved disciple, "My mother Mary is now your mother" (John19:26-27).

The point of this for those who are part of the family of God is that we are to honor and care for one another as members of the great family of God extending through time. We are all brothers and sisters, parents and children. God would have us live together as a family in the bond of Christian love. Yes, God himself is our father and Jesus is our brother. The bond cannot be broken.

Twenty-seven

To rest or not to rest

The disciples had just returned from a long and arduous trip proclaiming the good news that Jesus had entrusted to them. The days had been so full that there had hardly been enough time to eat. So, what was Jesus' response? "Being a missionary preacher is tough work, so buck up!" Well, not exactly. What he said is recorded in Mark 6:31 – "Obviously they were tired so I encouraged them to join me in a quiet place where they could rest."

What strikes me here is the importance of common sense not only in the ordinary issues of life, but in the more important as well. There was nothing more important than telling the people throughout Galilee that God's kingdom was breaking in. It was crucial that they learn about it, so doesn't that mean that every last ounce of energy and every remaining moment be used to spread the message? So we might think and in the contemporary world we would work at it all the harder (and probably solicit donations as well.) But Jesus said that they ought to find a quiet place and take a rest.

What does this suggest about how we are to carry out our responsibilities as ambassadors for

Christ? One thing that Jesus' instruction suggests is that God's kingdom doesn't depend, in an ultimate sense, on how diligently we carry out our part of the task.

Hard work pays off in earthly pursuits because, as a general rule most everything depends on us. Spend three or four extra hours on the job and we will earn more. Use every evening and every vacation working on "your book" and your fellow academicians will praise you for your contribution to knowledge in the field. Preach hard every Sunday and . . . . here it seems to break down because no longer does everything depend on our commitment to the task. Along with Paul we plant the seed, but it is God that makes it grow (1 Cor. 3:6). Jesus was pleased with the disciples' work, but more effort wasn't the key to success. It was God stepping in and making their seeds grow. He knows that our enthusiastic involvement is not the key when it comes to matters of the Spirit.

Interestingly enough, as they sailed away to the quiet place, the crowd got there first. When Jesus saw them "his heart went out to them . . . they were like sheep without a shepherd" (Mark 6:34). So the day was spent in teaching and healing and then at the end of the day Jesus fed 5,000 with nothing but five loaves and two fish. Sometimes the quiet time has to be postponed, but let it be Jesus who makes the recommendation.

Twenty-eight
Would Jesus enjoy a good party?

The question I keep asking myself is whether Jesus was as reserved and soft-spoken as we customarily think of him. The common view has Jesus mingling with the crowds, healing the sick and telling simple stories about how we are to live. And he did that. Wherever he went the crowds gathered to hear what he had to say, bringing their loved ones for healing. But is that all? Let's think about that for a moment. Perhaps the text will provide a clearer picture of his life among us? I'd like you to consider his encounter with the religious leaders as recorded in Matthew 15 and Mark 7.

One day some Pharisees and other religious authorities came to where Jesus was teaching. They noticed that his disciples had not washed their hands in the accepted ceremonially manner. One might expect that Jesus would quietly explain to them that people are not defiled from the outside, but from that which lies within. And he did, but not exactly in that reserved manner. He said, and I think he spoke with emphasis, "Isaiah was right when he prophesied about you hypocrites . . . you honor me with your lips but your hearts are far from me" (Matt. 15:7).

Does this not expand the customary view of how Jesus related to others? It's safe to say that it certainly raised the ire of the Jewish fundamentalists who were the targets of his criticism. The gentleness and humility that marked the life of Jesus (cf. Matt. 11:12-29) did not rule out the use of stronger language when appropriate. Immediately following this, the disciples went to him and asked for an explanation of what he meant by being "defiled from within." I have to think that the encounter with those he called hypocrites was still very much on his mind. In answer to the disciples' query he retorted, "Are you as dull as the others?" The words he chose reveal how he felt, do they not?

So what does his reaction in both of these settings infer about how we should live? For one thing, it encourages us to think of Jesus as more "human," than we normally do. Someday I really do want to hear Jesus laugh. I'm sure he did every time Peter came up with a new fish story. Why does goodness always have to be so saintly? We know that Jesus was fully God, but he was also fully human; he was "tempted in every way just as we are, yet without sin" (Heb. 4:15). To regard Jesus as one of us does not diminish his divinity in any way, but encourages us to embrace how completely human he was. I believe Jesus wants us to celebrate what it means to be a redeemed human being. Plaster of Paris Christianity has attracted very few to the faith.

Twenty-nine

Balancing priorities

Mark 7:24-30 records the story of Jesus as he traveled north out of Galilee into the seacoast area of Tyre and Sidon. The text tells us that he didn't want anyone to know where he was staying. Exactly why we don't know. Perhaps for a time of rest or perhaps because God the Father had planned that he meet a certain Syrophoenician woman whose daughter was demon possessed. In any case, when she rushed to him pleading for mercy for her daughter, he "gave her no answer, not a single word." A most unsuspected response for the one who had been spending so much time and energy doing that very thing.

The disciples, disturbed by the woman and the racket she was making, asked Jesus to get rid of her. He, however, turning to the woman explained that he had come to "help the lost sheep of Israel and no one else." She paid no attention, but fell at his feet and begged him to drive the evil spirit out of her daughter. Once again Jesus explained that his priority was to feed his own children, the Jews. He said, "It wouldn't be fair to take their bread and throw it to the dogs, the Gentiles."

Ouch! But she came back with, "But even the little dogs get to eat the scraps that fall from their master's table." Jesus couldn't help but respond to her remarkable faith, so he told her to return home where she would find her daughter healed. An unusual encounter! What can we possibly see in Jesus' actions and attitude that would help us to live a more Christ-like life?

What stands out for me is how focused Jesus was on his primary responsibility, that is, to tell his own people of the coming kingdom. Mark 1:5 records the first words of Jesus as he began his ministry – "The time has come. The kingdom of God has come near. Repent and believe the good news." Yet at the close of the story he acknowledged that "even the Gentiles" get to eat the scraps that fall from the table. Here we see the importance of maintaining focus while not neglecting the needs of others. Granted, that is hard to apply in life today. Obviously we know that our major responsibility as believers is to spread the message of salvation around the world (Matt. 28:19). What we can learn from Jesus' encounter with the Syrophoenician woman is that in this task we are not to overlook the practical needs of others along the way.

Thirty

The secondary role of healing

In the story of the healing of the deaf mute (Matt. 15) we can't help but notice the difference between what was important for Jesus and what interested the crowd. Jesus had gone up from the seacoast to the hill country in order to teach the crowds. They, however, were more interested in his power to heal. So they brought to him all who were in need of physical healing. His major concern was to inform the mind and heart – theirs was to heal the body. One person they brought to Jesus was a man who could neither speak nor hear. When it came time to heal him, Jesus took the man away from the crowd. The people crowded after him anyway. As soon as the deaf mute was cured Jesus told them not to tell anyone about what had happened. They paid no attention and began to spread the news everywhere. What we see here are two distinct priorities. Jesus wanted to teach; they wanted him to heal. Jesus wanted to be alone with the deaf mute; they wanted to watch the healing. Jesus wanted them not to tell others about what he had done; they did it anyway. There is no question but that their concerns were different from those of Jesus.

What does this suggest about living a Christ-like

life? One thing is the importance of maintaining focus on that which is of eternal importance. It's wonderful that the poor man was cured so that for the remaining years he could hear and speak. That was a concern for Jesus. But think of the eternal consequences of hearing and accepting the good news that the kingdom of God had come! The prospect of such a magnificent reality was a higher priority for Jesus.

But why did Jesus insist that the crowd not tell others what had happened? The answer is that he did not want healing to be considered as the focus of his ministry. People are naturally attracted to the sensational. There may be a warning here for the prominent role of music in today's worship service. It is scripture that must continue absolutely central and not sidelined by that which is best understood as supportive. Both/and is good theory, but the balance tends to shift quite regularly away from what is truly important.

Thirty-one

To forget yourself – watch Jesus

In Matthew 15 we have the story of Jesus feeding the 4,000. What impresses me is the way Jesus continued to take the initiative. He called his disciples together, he expressed sorrow for the plight of those needing food, he asked his disciples about available loaves and fish, he told the crowd to sit down, he took the little they had, he gave thanks, he broke the bread into pieces and gave it to the disciples to be distributed. Jesus was the one definitely in charge. Had he not taken the initiative, it would have been quite a different story. What can we learn from the way Jesus responded to a crowd away from home and hungry? One thing is that we are to be acutely aware of the needs of others. The developing problem may have passed through the minds of several of the disciples, but since the answer wasn't obvious, it was dismissed. They supported their inaction arguing that they were in a desolate place, and there was no way to get any food. (Never mind that just a short time before they watched Jesus turn five loaves of bread and two little fish into enough food to feed 5,000 men, to say nothing of the women and children who would have been there.

That Jesus assumed leadership in this situation is important. Over the years I have tended to think of him more as responding to need than initiating action. I had the feeling that he was there to do the right thing rather than to trigger action.

Obviously there needs to be a balance, but at least on this occasion if Jesus hadn't taken the initiative the 4,000 would have gone away hungry. What the account suggests is that living like Jesus requires us to be increasingly aware of the needs of others and how they can be met. It is all part of the life-long reversal of self- concern that ought to be taking place in the heart of every true believer. One problem with self-absorption is that it blinds us to the needs of others. To be like Jesus is to get over self and step up to the challenge of caring for the other. That's what Jesus did from his first day of public ministry all the way to that last day on the cross. And it is what we do as well if we are following him.

No one is brought to Christ because of what we do. Our role is to proclaim the message; it is God who draws sinners home. I believe this is the model Jesus left for us.

Thirty-two
The hard edge of truth

Jesus had just delivered what we now refer to as the Bread of Life discourse. The conclusion was, "Whoever eats my body and drinks my blood has eternal life" (John 6:54). Many of his followers found this offensive and questioned if anyone could accept it. Jesus response was not to restate his point in softer language, but to give them what one might call a you-haven't-seen-anything-yet answer. If his teaching on the bread of life had been offensive, then how would they handle his ascension into heaven (John 6:62). He added that some of them really believed and it was because the Father had made it possible. At this point many of his so-called followers abandoned him.

What does this tell us about Jesus that is relevant to how his followers today should conduct themselves? One thing is that he would not bend the truth in order to gain or maintain a following. Perhaps the greatest weakness of the contemporary church is its willingness to adjust the message (at least, the way it is presented) with the hope of gaining numbers.

That would have been foreign to Jesus. I believe he would applaud Justice Scalia who counseled, "Have the courage to have your wisdom regarded as stupidity. Be fools for Christ. And have the courage to suffer the contempt of the sophisticated world."

Jesus' reaction to his followers taking offense was not to find a way to bridge the gap caused by truth. While his apparent lack of concern at the moment could be questioned by some, there comes a time when we simply hold truth to be true. I am not suggesting a belligerent defense, but a simple acceptance of the fact that truth by its nature rules out falsehood. Could that be embarrassing? Certainly. Could it separate? Yes, but it is one of the difficult tasks of life to be done with determination. But isn't determination simply an expectation of any secular code of ethics? Many years ago Bonaparte said, "Resolute determination is the truest wisdom." Long before that, Buddha taught that the sure way to reach Nirvana was to "walk the eightfold noble path with unswerving determination."

So in what way is determination a Christian ethic? And the answer is, In no special way if you are talking about an ethic that belongs solely to the Christian faith. The vast majority of ethical maxims in the western world are equally applicable in both worlds. The interesting fact is that the so-called secular code of western civilization is based on the Judeo-Christian ethic clearly stated in the biblical record. It is not by accident that we in the west enjoy a level of moral expectation that honors women, responds to humanitarian needs, and plays a major role in that which is beneficial to all.

Jesus faced his coming test with determination. Hebrews says that he was "tempted in every way, just as we are – yet he did not sin" (4:15). In the garden of Gethsemane he wrestled with the decision. With tears he pled, "Abba, Father, everything is possible for you. Take this cup from me," yet concluded, "Not what I will, but what you will (Mark 14:36). Jesus' determination becomes our model for what it means in life to face every difficult choice with a conviction that remains firm to the very end.

Thirty-three

Tips from a mountaintop

That the account of the transfiguration is recorded in all three Synoptic gospels suggests its importance in the early church. Let's review the story, noting what Jesus did, in order to learn how we can become more like him. Granted, this is a special occasion (God speaks from heaven identifying Jesus as his son) and not one in which we are liable to find ourselves.

The first thing is that he went to a high mountain where, in his words, "he could be alone." If the Son of God needs an occasional break, it probably isn't necessary that the contemporary pastor be on call 24/7. What we often view as commitment could well be personal desire to achieve, an expression of pride. What Jesus is saying to the task-driven minister is, "Time for a high mountain experience where being alone will bring renewal."

While Jesus was praying he was transfigured and two Old Testament notables joined him in that glorious setting to discuss his coming death and resurrection. Wouldn't you know it, "Peter, James, and John had grown sleepy." But not a word of censure from their leader, not even when Peter suggested memorializing the event by building shrines. Jesus recognized that Peter was missing the true glory of the event, still thinking in earthly terms, but no words of rebuke are recorded. Being like Jesus calls us to overlook the failure of others. There is a time for proper instruction, but there is also a time to skip it.

One last thing: When the disciples heard the voice of God from heaven, they fell to the ground overcome with fear. Had Jesus been one of us, he may have said, "Serves them right. First, they missed the transfiguration being asleep; second, when they woke up, Peter offered a very secular idea; and finally, when God spoke from heaven they lost control and fell to the ground." But Jesus "stepped forward and touched them" saying, "Stand to your feet; don't be afraid." Once again we see that quiet gentleness with which he mentored his own. In this incident, which involved such a unique display of heavenly glory, he continued to lovingly guide his disciples in a way that would be most helpful.

So here are three things we can learn from Jesus: take it easy now and then, resist correcting the other, love them anyway.

Thirty-four

Why was Jesus a good teacher?

On the road to Damascus the disciples began arguing about which one of them would be the greatest in the coming kingdom. Perhaps Peter argued his enthusiasm, John his insight into spiritual matters, and Judas Iscariot his ability to handle finances. In any case, once inside the house Jesus asked them what they were discussing along the way. Of course, they were embarrassed and didn't answer. So Jesus sat down and taught them exactly what they needed to learn at that point – the road to greatness leads through the valley of humility. Taking a little child into his arms, Jesus explained that even to enter the kingdom they would have to become as humble as that little one. True greatness is humility, becoming the least.

While the words of Jesus explain how a believer should live, I would like to reflect on what Jesus did as part of the disciples' learning experience. First, he was aware of what they were talking about, but didn't butt in to tell them how wrong they were. He waited until they were indoors where there would be less distraction; then he raised the question about their discussion along the way. Here we see the careful consideration of a master teacher. So often our zeal to show that we have the answer leads to a poor job in conveying the truth.

Another thing I notice is that it is Jesus who takes the initiative. Mark 9:35 says that Jesus sat down and "called the Twelve" to come and listen. Most people do not like to confront. Friends continue for years, each with a detrimental habit that could have been lovingly confronted to their advantage. I know that "unsolicited advice is criticism," but most of us will remember having received from a friend some helpful word of correction. To "be like Jesus" is to help others see their blind spots in a gracious and loving fashion?

The other observation is that Jesus used a most effective method of teaching. They would never forget a child in his arms as he taught them a lesson in humility. Rote memory is fine for storing away necessary facts, but when it comes to teaching how to live, there is nothing quite like a living example.

Thirty-five

Determination

Jesus realized that the time to return to heaven was drawing near so he set out for Jerusalem "determined to carry out his role" (Luke 9:51). He went through a Samaritan village, but the people wouldn't receive him because it was clear to them that he was "determined to go on to Jerusalem" (vv. 52-53). It is clear from these verses that Jesus was totally committed to the task assigned to him by the Father. He had come into the world to lay down his life as a redemptive sacrifice and now the time had come. He was focused on that crucial event soon to happen. He was determined to get to Jerusalem and determined to carry out his role.

What we see here is a remarkable personal commitment to a redemptive task that goes way beyond our ability to imagine. God had assigned him the task of bearing the sins of the world, and he was determined to carry it out. Since Jesus is the model for Christian living, what does this say about how we are to live? Obviously, we are to approach the difficult tasks of life with determination as he did. But isn't determination simply an expectation of any secular code of ethics? Many years ago Bonaparte said, "Resolute determination is the truest wisdom."

Long before that, Buddha taught that the sure way to reach Nirvana was to "walk the eightfold noble path with unswerving determination." So in what way is determination a Christian ethic? And the answer is, In no special way if you are talking about an ethic that belongs solely to the Christian faith. The vast majority of ethical maxims in the western world are equally applicable in both worlds. The interesting fact is that the so-called secular code of western civilization is based on the Judea-Christian ethic clearly stated in the biblical record. It is not by accident that we in the west enjoy a level of moral expectation that honors women, responds to humanitarian needs, and plays a major role in that which is beneficial to all.

Jesus faced his coming test with determination. Hebrews says that he was "tempted in every way, just as we are – yet he did not sin" (4:15). In the garden of Gethsemane he wrestled with the decision. With tears he pled, "Abba, Father, everything is possible for you. Take this cup from me," yet concluded, "Not what I will, but what you will" (Mark 14:36). Jesus' determination becomes our model for what it means in life to face every difficult choice with a conviction that remains firm to the very end.

Thirty-six

Lessons from Bethany

In the previous blog we noted now determined Jesus was to get to Jerusalem. Before him lay a task that was absolutely central to his mission – carrying through with the unimaginable sacrifice of his life for the sins of the world. I can see him as he walks with firm step, eyes fixed on the goal ahead. But arriving at Bethany he stops and spends time with two women, sisters of his dear friend Lazarus. What we can take away from this is the importance of friendships. They must remain a high priority. All too often the busyness of life demands way too much of our time and energy.

The way in which Jesus conducted himself on that passing visit teaches another important lesson. It was Mary who sat quietly at his feet absorbing all he had to say while Martha busied herself preparing a meal. Upset with her sister, Martha burst into the room and accused Jesus of not caring that Mary was not helping in the kitchen.

With love, Jesus said to the rather frustrated hostess: "Martha, dear Martha, you worry and fret about so many things" (Luke 10:41). One can sense the gentleness of his voice and demeanor. Forget for the moment her accusation that he didn't care. Jesus took the high road, correcting Martha in love and pointing out that Mary, who according to Martha, was neglecting her responsibility, had actually made the better choice.

What I see here is the willingness to confront in love. When we feel that we have done the right thing it is hard to extend a cordial hand to the one who has critiqued us unfairly. Part of love is the willingness to accept the criticism of those who are convinced they are right. That is what Jesus did and he is our example of how to live like a "Christian."

Thirty-seven

Was Jesus confrontational?

Luke records the story of Jesus in confrontation with the religious authorities of his day. A Pharisee had invited Jesus home for dinner and was surprised when his guest did not wash his hands before eating. That was a Jewish custom and, if not followed, would have made a person ceremonially unclean. That Jesus did not follow this practice was not what they had expected. Instead, he corrected them very severely saying that although they cleansed the outside, inside they were full of extortion and wickedness. Then he went on to speak of their lack of justice and their habit of demanding respect in the marketplace. Far from being ceremonially pure, they were like "unmarked graves" that polluted anyone who stepped on them. They realized they were being insulted, so they turned hostile. As Jesus left, they tagged along behind trying to trap him in his speech. When you read the entire account in Luke 11:37-54 you see how confrontational Jesus was on this occasion. After all, he was a guest at a dinner party. Was that the proper time to say to the religious authorities, "You fools!" and, "Woe to you, Pharisees"! Putting the other person on the defense creates an awkward moment at a dinner party.

Is Jesus teaching us how we are to conduct ourselves in similar situations? Or should we exercise a bit more restraint? Perhaps we should follow his example when he is doing nice helpful things, but not when the situation calls for opposition? No, that can't be right. It would leave us the option of doing only what we wanted to do. I believe the answer is to take a careful look at the principle that lies behind the action. Context is crucial. The way Jesus handled the situation indicates how serious it is to turn the worship of a holy God into a vast collection of legalistic rules. To drive home this point called for some very direct language. The fact that the Scribes and Pharisees were so well versed in the religious status quo made it all the more difficult. When we meet a somewhat similar situation our goal should not be to use the same words, but to accomplish the same result.

Thirty-eight

Jesus was no legalist

Everyone knows that in the days of Jesus the Jewish people lived by a very strict set of rules. Some people belonged to a sect called the Pharisees, which means "separated." The idea was to be completely separate from sin by strict obedience to an extensive collection of legal instructions designed to keep members from breaking any one of the cardinal laws of scripture. The outcome of such a repressive religious system was pride and hypocrisy. Since perfection is unattainable, the practice couldn't help but lead to hypocrisy.

One Sabbath, Jesus was teaching in a synagogue when a woman, crippled eighteen years by a demon, came in. Jesus called her over and touched her bent back. Instantly she stood erect and began to praise God. The synagogue leader was indignant and pontificated that it was improper to heal on the Sabbath. (Plenty of weekdays for things like that!) Jesus denounced them as hypocrites, pointing out that since they watered their animals on the Sabbath, surely he could set a daughter of Abraham free on that day. The Pharisees were embarrassed, but the crowd was overjoyed. So the question is – How do we live like that?

Granted, we are not in the business of expelling demons on Sunday, but what can we learn from the way Jesus conducted himself? One thing is that he called hypocrisy for what it is. Understanding the duplicity of human nature, he pointed out the hypocrisy of those who abuse their power. I believe followers of Christ should not grow insensitive to social maladies. There are congressmen to write to and marches to join. Our home may be in heaven, but it is this present world in which are living for now. Another thing is that Jesus argued quite convincingly to make his case. Can we not give thought to the inequities of today's world and think how we can effectively enter the discussion? And finally, he cared about a woman crippled for life and did something about it. Yes, I think we can follow his example.

Thirty-nine

Steadfast toward the goal

Having healed the woman on the Sabbath, Jesus "continued going through towns and villages, always teaching, as he pressed on toward Jerusalem" (Luke 13:22.) The word that comes to mind is constancy, that "quality of being unchanging or unwavering, as in purpose, love, or loyalty." Jesus "continued" on his mission, he was "always" teaching, and he "pressed on" toward Jerusalem. In short, he displayed a remarkable constancy. No issues of secondary importance derailed his steadfast commitment to what was central.

Luke pictures Jesus going through one town after another, teaching and healing as he went. Certainly the families of those he had healed would have been delighted to have him stay a bit longer in each town along the way, but a cross was waiting for him in Jerusalem. With his eye fixed firmly on that goal, he moved steadily forward.

So how should this quality be seen in the lives of us who in the 21st century claim to be following him? Certainly we need to get our priorities in order. Why are we here and what does God want us to be doing? There is nothing wrong with the "Caribbean cruises" of life, but one has to guard against the non-essential replacing what is strategically important for our Lord.

And while we are moving along the particular route that God has laid out for us, let's be sure we keep moving. We may be tempted to stay in town A because it is such a pleasant place, but town B is waiting for what God wants to do through us there. Each stage in life has its own unique opportunity so let's not dillydally.

Forty

Courage for a time of crisis

It is now late in Jesus' ministry and he is on his way to Jerusalem. Hear him as he tells the story.

"Just then some Pharisees came up and warned me to leave because Herod Antipas was laying plans to kill me. I told them, 'Go and tell that fox that for the time being I intend to continue my work of casting out demons and healing the sick; after that I will go to Jerusalem and complete my mission. Indeed, in spite of your plans to harm me, I must continue my journey to Jerusalem because, as you have heard it said, 'It is impossible for a prophet to die outside of Jerusalem'" (Luke 13:31- 33).

The character quality that stands out to me in this incident is courage. The Roman governor was both cruel and resourceful. That he was making plans to kill someone would normally strike fear in the heart of the victim. The various methods used by Rome to do away with their enemies were extremely brutal. But Jesus did not cringe. He simply told the anxious messengers to tell Antipas that he intended to continue his ministry and then go to Jerusalem to carry out his mission. He even chided them with their own saying that Hebrew prophets have to die in Jerusalem.

Right now we live in a time of international terror. We hear of atrocities taking place around the world and we wonder how we might react if called upon to make that decisive choice. Jesus knew he was carrying out a destiny planned for him. It would involve the humility and pain of a public crucifixion, yet he continued on the path assigned by the Father.

Does not each believer have a mission to fulfill? I believe so. Could it involve martyrdom? Yes. Will it? Only God knows. The one thing we do know is that, like Jesus, we are to demonstrate the courage that comes from absolute trust in the will of God. Anxiety changes not a thing; instead, it robs us of the joy of the moment. And where does that necessary courage come from? It is certainly in that group of virtues mentioned by Paul in his second letter to Timothy where he tells his young helper, "God has not given us a spirit of fear and timidity, but of power, love, and self-discipline" (1:7). God alone is the source of all courage.

Forty-one

Jesus send the lepers to a priest?

As Jesus passes through a village on his final trip to
Jerusalem ten men with leprosy call out for help. He
stops for a moment and says, "Go to the priests and
let them examine you" (Luke 17:14). What strikes me
here is that Jesus is directing the lepers to go to that
very group of religious leaders who had given him so
much trouble. When they ridiculed him for his position
on wealth he reminded them that while they may have
convinced the crowd that they were righteous, God
could read their hearts and he found them "loathsome
in his sight" (Luke 16:15). And now he tells the lepers
to go to those very priests to be declared ceremonially
clean. Why would he do that? Wasn't he the one who
came to replace their corrupt distortion of the ancient
religion with a new understanding of the love of God?

Some might say it was his method of proving his
adversaries wrong. They didn't appreciate his ministry
and had actively opposed everything he was doing.
That the deaf could now hear and the blind see was of
no particular importance to religious leaders who had
surrendered to self-indulgence. So when the lepers
appeared before the priests cured of their disease, his
antagonists would have to admit that Jesus could do

something way beyond their meager abilities. But does this scenario seem likely in view of the Jesus pictured elsewhere in the gospels? Hardly.

So what is happening? Why did Jesus send them to the temple? I believe it's because Jesus had not come establish a new religion, but to fulfill the historic religion of his people. Never in his teaching had he suggested that the history of Abraham or the laws of Moses were something of the past and needed to be replaced with his new insights. It is true that in the course of history Christianity has come to be considered by some as unrelated to Judaism. But Christ is not the new leader showing a new way; he is the promised Messiah of the Old Testament.

Christianity fulfills the hopes and religious aspirations of the tribes of Israel. What we call the "New" Testament is the fulfillment, not the replacement, of the "Old" Testament. I believe that what Jesus rejected was the hypocrisy and distortion of their sacred religion, not its essence. And for that reason it was appropriate for the lepers to go to the priest. It was the accepted way of being recognized as a renewed member of a religious society.

Forty-two

Getting ahead by waiting

Not long ago I wrote of the courage of Jesus as he made his way toward Jerusalem. The text says that he "set his face" toward his destination (Luke 9:51, 53). He was determined to get there even though the authorities were waiting in Jerusalem to take his life. Yet we read that on a different occasion he "remained in Galilee," not wanting to go to Jerusalem because the religious authorities there were determined to kill him (John 7:1). Sounds like after thinking it over, he decided not to run the risk. However, as the following verses tell us, he did go up a day or so later when "his time had fully come" (vv. 8, 10). You will remember that his brothers had been urging him to go to Jerusalem so that more of his followers could see the miracles he was doing. But Jesus waited until it was the right time for him to go. It wasn't the opposition of the authorities that kept him in Galilee for a time, but an awareness that everything has its own time. He was waiting for that right time.

Is there a lesson here for us? Is there a right time, from God's standpoint, for us to do a certain thing? I believe so. In ordaining our life, God has laid out a specific track for us to follow. We don't expect a child to go to college just out of grade school; we know that there are several years of maturing that need to take place. Perhaps God sees that same need in our life and has us wait for the time being. Waiting is probably the most difficult task for today's busy person. We are used to getting a thing done by just doing it. Don't bother with preparation. (I understand it was a surprise for Nike to discover that their iconic slogan "Just do it" had its origin in the dying words of an infamous murderer.) In any case, most of us have a hard time waiting for God to tell us what HIS next step is for us. He doesn't seem to be in as much of a hurry as we are.

Jesus was content to wait in Galilee (continuing his ministry of course) until the Father told him it was okay to go. For us to conduct our life like Jesus on this occasion is to keep on doing what God has assigned until he says, "Now is the right time for you to take that next step." And how will we know if that "voice" is God's or someone else's? In my experience if a person has been listening to Him on a regular basis they are more able to distinguish his voice at that moment when they need guidance. In his letter to the Philippians, Paul tells the believers, "If on some point you think differently, God will make it clear to you" (3:15). So wait till he says the time has come, then move ahead. The neat part is that if you are making a mistake he has promised to make that clear to you. You will reach your goal more quickly if you don't waste your time running down dead ends.

Forty-three

How to handle controversy

One of the encounters of Jesus with the religious authorities is found in John 10:22-39. This one took place at the Feast of Dedication in Jerusalem toward the end of Jesus' ministry. As I have mentioned, my purpose in the Jesus blogs is to learn how he acted in various situations, not what he said. In this short encounter he demonstrates several ways that we should respond if we find ourselves in a similar situation. First the story, then the lessons.

Walking one day in Solomon's Porch, the authorities "cornered" Jesus to ask how much longer he intended to "provoke them" as he was doing (v. 24). He responded very directly, saying that his works proved that he was who he said he was – "I and the Father are one." At that, the priests picked up stones in order to kill him (v. 31), but instead of cowering he boldly asked for which of his good works were they about to stone him (v. 32). They countered saying that it wasn't because of what he was doing, but because he claimed to be God – and that was blasphemy. His defense was that scripture spoke of people as "gods" so apparently his assertion couldn't be considered blasphemy? (vv. 34-36). Nonplussed by this argument, they tried once again to arrest him, but he "escaped out of their grasp" (v. 39).

One thing we learn from Jesus in this confrontation is that we are to live without fear. Everything he did provoked the religious leadership. While he didn't go out of his way to offend them, his message showed them up for the hypocrites they were. Although it was forbidden for them to kill anyone – only Rome could do that – they were so disturbed that they actually picked up stones to kill him.

A second thing to notice is how wise Jesus was in the exchange. Every good debater knows how critical it is to put the other person on defense. So Jesus asked for which of the helpful deeds he had recently done did they intend to kill him. It is clear that you don't kill a person for the good they do, and they realized that they were caught in their own trap. Then he undermined their argument that he had committed blasphemy by claiming to be one with God because the scripture, which they held to be without error, spoke of some people as "gods." Just good solid reasoning and they were supposed to be the experts in that field.

Finally, when they tried to at arrest him he "escaped from their grasp." Most commentators see this as divine intervention. Jesus knew that God the Father was involved in every step along his way and would not allow anything to happen that was outside of his will. So the three guiding principles that are seen in this encounter are for us to (1) live without fear, (2) meet opposition intelligently, and (3) rest secure in our confidence that God is in control. Put more succinctly: Be unafraid, be informed, trust him.

Forty-four

Did Jesus actually weep?

Many years ago when I was teaching a college freshman class in New Testament Survey, I had a student tell me that since Jesus was God there was nothing he didn't know or couldn't do. I pressed him a bit and learned that when Jesus was a baby he just pretended not to know since that would be hard to explain to others. The student didn't know it, but he was involved in what theologians call the "hypostatic union" – the doctrine of the two natures of the incarnate Jesus (divine and human). It stems from the time of Athanasius (a fourth century bishop of Alexandria) and was adopted as orthodox at the Council of Chalcedon in 451. In simple terms, the student didn't want his Jesus to be like the rest of us. It amounted to a denial of the humanity of Christ.

While informed believers accept the doctrine of two natures, there is at the same time a tendency to view Jesus as essentially divine and only acting like a man from time to time. In the account of the raising of Lazarus (John 11:1-44) I notice several very human reactions – things that you and I might do, but not characteristic of how we might view a divine being. Jesus had heard that his dear friend Lazarus was ill so after two days he decided to go to Judea to see him. The fact that he waited two days has furrowed many a brow, but one thing is for sure, it's more like man than God. The text says that Jesus "loved Martha, her sister Mary, and Lazarus" (v. 5). The mention of each person emphasizes his love for each one individually; the imperfect tense in the Greek text suggests a continuing state. Since Jesus was both man and God, which one did the loving? Or was it both?

Later in the account, when Jesus saw Mary and her friends weeping, he was "deeply moved in spirit and visibly distressed" (v. 33). A moment later when they invited him to come and see the body, he "burst into tears" (v. 35). Once again I ask, was it God himself incarnate that couldn't control his tears, or was it Jesus the man? I am not a theologian, but I understand that even today there is a difference in opinion on this issue between the Reformed and the Lutheran traditions. The important point for us is that Jesus cared. His concern for a dear brother taken so quickly, affected him deeply: He wept (v. 35, the shortest verse in the New Testament.)

I do not believe in sentimentality, but the way Jesus lived tells us not to fortress ourselves against an honest expression of emotion whenever appropriate. To care for the welfare of a friend facing death may move us to follow the lead of Jesus and give way to tears. While some have thought that Jesus' tears were due to the gloomy sense of loss prevalent at the moment, I choose to understand them as the tears of "one who has been tempted in every way, just as we are – yet he did not sin" (Heb. 4:15).

Forty-five

How to "Seize the moment"

On one occasion, the wife of Zebedee, with her two sons, James and John, in tow, approached Jesus with a rather audacious question (Mark 10:35-45). She asked Jesus if, when his kingdom came, could her sons be seated one on each side. When the other disciples heard what was going on they became highly indignant. And rightly so. So how did Jesus use this occasion? That is the question. The text goes on to say that he "called them all together" (v. 42) and taught them a very important lesson. Ruling over others and vaunting one's authority is the way this world works, but not the way in God's kingdom. In the spiritual kingdom if you want to be a leader, then serve the other person, don't insist on being served. Then Jesus used himself as an example. The Son of Man came to serve, not to be served – and that would ultimately involve death on a cross.

What strikes me here is that Jesus recognized and took advantage of the right moment. The two disciples and their mother had created a situation that was ripe for teaching a particular lesson that needed to be learned. The two disciples were exposed by their inappropriate request for power, the other disciples displayed their disgust, and Jesus did what the well-known Latin saying (slightly adjusted) suggests, *Carpe momentum*: he seized the moment, that passing moment so highly suitable for learning. The moment for calling them together had come and the master teacher did not let it slip by.

I am sure that those responsible for the growth of others understand that certain instructions are best shared only when "the moment" has arrived. Since all instruction is based on the necessary assumption that there are things you don't know but need to, informing the other needs to be carried out in a non-judgmental manner. The parent responsible for the spiritual nurture of the child is more effective if they choose the "right moment" to help a child understand some important lesson about growing up. The believer concerned about the spiritual welfare of a friend is more effective if they wait for the "right moment" – the moment that God has in mind for the believer to share the need for spiritual rebirth. The truth is that God would have us work according to his schedule and those right moments often come unexpectedly. So stay sensitive to the One who has prepared the heart of the other, and being a gentleman, doesn't shout out his orders.

Forty-six

Surrounded by need – so?

The purpose of this book on Jesus is to learn what he did in various situations rather than listen to what he taught. It may be possible to learn certain things from the way he reacts that are not necessarily expressed in his teachins. So let's watch as one day he leaves Jericho with his disciples. A blind beggar by the name of Bartimaeus hears the crowd that so often accompanied Jesus and calls out for pity. It is interesting how the synoptists record the moment: When Bartimaeus kept calling for help, some in the crowd were upset and insisted that he be silenced (Mark 10 gives the fullest account), but Jesus "stopped" (v. 49) and asked that the man in need be brought to him.

The crowd was "passing by," but Jesus "stopped" – and there is the difference between the heart of God and the nature of man. One might argue that both the disciples and the followers needed to learn all that Jesus had to teach and that there would undoubtedly have been other times to take care of a blind man. Certainly the needs of the many outweigh the need of a single person. So goes the warped reasoning of the mind turned inward for personal gain.

But life is not a zero-sum game and acts of kindness expand their domain without limiting others.

The lesson that the crowd was to learn was presented with far more impact by illustrating it than by discussing it. Had Jesus said something about it being a fine thing to heal the blind, lives would probably never have been changed. But to actually see him respond to a need he could meet would leave an indelible impression. In the long run, learning has less to do with the accumulation of information than it has with the doing of what we "know." When it comes to moral choice, we "know" what we do, not what we remember.

Granted, we don't meet many physically blind people today and if we did there is not a lot that we ourselves could do about it? But we are constantly surrounded by people with other kinds of blindness. Some cannot "see" the gospel as the story of God's redemptive love for them. Others have never "seen" the beneficial results of caring for the needy, the insights of scripture for a more satisfying life, that apart from God there is no hope. We are surrounded by blindness and like Bartimaeus, they are calling for help. If God has opened our eyes through faith in Jesus Christ we know the one thing that needs to be "seen" by all who would prepare for an eternity in heaven. Others may pass by the needy, but let's stop along with Jesus and meet the immediate need.

Forty-seven

Why Jesus wept

Jesus was nearing Jerusalem on his final journey and as he came up over a sudden rise the famous city stretched out before him. Luke writes that Jesus "broke into tears" (19:41) and adds that the Lord's sorrow for the city was that those who lived there didn't know what made for peace. It was a classic "if only this, then that" situation. Had they known the way of peace there would have been no destruction. But in the year AD 79 the Romans sacked the city and desecrated the holy temple. Jesus wept for the city because of what would happen in a few years, but didn't need to. He broke into tears, moved by the realization that the coming fall of Jerusalem wasn't necessary.

That which catches my attention is Jesus' reaction to an avoidable tragedy. It is enough that the city would be destroyed, but what made it worse was the fact that it didn't need to happen. When we see human suffering that is unnecessary, how do we react? "Serves them right; they had it coming," or "How sad because it didn't have to happen?" Jesus wept, not simply because of what in time would take place, but because it was not inevitable.

So I ask, how can this perspective be integrated into the mindset of today's Christian believer? If we would be more like Jesus, one thing is that we would give increasing attention to the Why of tragedy. While it is helpful to take part in restoration of the damage, a more important need is to discover why it happened and make the change there.

In one of his beatitudes, Jesus said, "Blessed are those who understand the sorrow of this world, for God himself will comfort and encourage them" (Matt. 5:4). To understand that all suffering and heartache of every sort in our world is the result of sin, gives us the starting point for renewal. We will spend less time taking care of results and more on prevention. Wherever God is honored and his teaching is adopted, the climate for a meaningful and happy life is increased. Looking out over our Jerusalem, may we join the Master and be moved to tears at the devastation that doesn't need to happen. Then, of course, we redouble our efforts to discover the why and take the necessary action.

Forty-eight
Cleansing "temples"

Before there was a New Testament (as a composite of apostolic letters), early believers were encouraged to watch how their leaders lived, and then imitate their faith (Heb. 13:7). For example, Paul urged the believers at Corinth to "imitate" him (1 Cor. 4:16). Throughout history believers have been challenged to reflect on the way they live, on what it means to be a child of God. What I have been doing in these blogs on Jesus is to watch how he acted in various life situations and suggest how that should work out in our 21st century world. I knew that before long I would arrive at that dramatic moment when Jesus entered the temple and saw how religious leaders had turned it into a commercial enterprise. It is one of the very few episodes that occurs in all four gospels.

What met the eyes of Jesus when he went into the Court of the Gentiles was appalling; animals were being sold for sacrifice, money was being exchanged, God's "house of prayer" had been turned into a "hideout for thieves."

So Jesus took some pieces of cord, twisted them into a whip and began to drive the animals out of the Court. He turned the tables of the money changes upside down scattering coins in every direction. "How dare you turn my Father's house into a market place!" he demanded. One thing we must accept and that is that he did it in a "Christ like" manner. I know, that is a strange picture, but Jesus was the Christ whose life we are called upon to imitate. I ask, How does this work out today? What are the "temples" we are to cleanse, the demands we are to make, the zeal for righteousness that stirs us to action?

The first thing to find out is what exactly was it was that he was opposing. It is clear that the religious leaders were profaning the house of God and using it as a source of revenue. They were secularizing the sacred. Do we see something like that going on today? At the risk of alienating some, I would suggest that the "worship service" of many a contemporary church is, for all purposes, a secular musical concert employing Christian words. I see little difference between the musical score of the service and what was happening the night before at a local rock concert. Both are highly emotive, designed to create a certain sensation, and anything but worshipful in the traditional sense.

Worship is an awareness of the presence of Almighty God, perfect in love, righteousness and power. I do not find this in what passes as sacred music today. We are all familiar with the role of music in supporting the scene in a movie. Light and happy music says one thing, a slow sensuous beat, something else. Each plays its distinct role. But the God I know, if he needs a musical setting, is great beyond words, infinitely pure and righteous, kind beyond description. How should he be represented musically?

Back to my point about application. When I enter the "temple" of church music, do I take a whip and drive out the musicians, upset the communion table and demand that the organist play Bach only? Would that be Christ like? Why not? I am going to leave the answer open to you, yet suggest that it should not remain open for good. And should we agree on an answer to that "temple activity that may need cleansing," what can be said about the host of other related areas?

Forty-nine

To speak or not to speak?

There is a wonderful story of Jesus and the religious authorities that is included in all four gospels. It takes place during his final ministry in Jerusalem. The authorities demanded that Jesus tell them by what authority he was doing what he did. Jesus answered by asking them whether John the Baptist's authority to baptize came from heaven or from men. Either option would get them in trouble, so they claimed they didn't know. Jesus responded, "Since you won't answer my question, neither will I answer yours" (Matt. 21:27).

What stands out to me is the way Jesus confronted his opposition. He did not let them diminish him by playing the old social status card (they being superior by virtue of their role in society). After all, he was just a commoner from a little village further north. When it came to intellectual acumen he won the debate (if we may call it that) by putting them in a position where they couldn't answer. There was no way out.

How does this technique apply to us? Some might think that the believer should adopt the meek and mild approach and accept the world's disdain. That certainly isn't what Jesus did. He stood up to the authorities and discussed the issue with them as an equal. He outwitted them at their own game. But isn't that pretty self-centered? Not if Jesus did it, and he did. Of course, so much depends on the way "conflict" is carried out. We might try to play the role and find ourselves acting in a purely secular way. But Jesus showed us that it was possible to confront where necessary and do it in a Christian way.

I believe it's important to remember that having accepted Christ as savior, we are actually . . . children of God. Don't let that slip off your tongue as if it had little relevance. We are the sons and daughters of a God who created out of nothing all that is, who spoke and the universe came into existence. That's who we are! Stand tall, not boasting, but fully aware of who we are in Him. With this attitude let's face the moment calmly, knowing that God will provide the resources necessary for the occasion. Jesus wants winners, not wall flowers.

Fifty

Trapping people into seeing their error

On one occasion Jesus told a parable about a landowner who leased his vineyard to some vine growers and left on a long journey. Upon returning he sent some servants to collect his share of the profit. The tenants seized the servants, beat some and killed others. So the owner sent a larger group of servants and they were treated the same way. Finally he sent his only son and the tenants, thinking they would inherit the vineyard, killed the son. Jesus asked the religious leaders how they thought the owner would respond and they were sure that he would "put those scoundrels to a miserable death" (Matt. 21:41). Then as the conversation continued, the Pharisees "began to realize that he was talking about them" (v. 45). Caught in their own trap, they didn't follow through with their plan to take him into custody because they were afraid of the crowds who regarded Jesus as a prophet.

The Greek text says that Jesus was talking *pros autous*, which would normally be translated "to them," but the preposition can be understood in a number of ways depending on context. Of the several possibilities it could mean "in reference to" or "against," either of which would and did, offend the religious legalist. Jesus wanted the Pharisees to understand that their religious practices were morally unacceptable. Interestingly enough, he didn't just tell them, but led them down a path where they came to that conclusion themselves.

Here's my question: What can we learn from Jesus' decision to tell this parable even though he knew it would offend a portion of his audience? What does it imply for us who are to live as he did? If Jesus is our mentor then we ought to be reflecting more and more on those ways of thinking and acting that he displayed. That he wasn't afraid to speak his mind, is clear (obviously he did it in the right way). That he was concerned to correct religious hypocrisy is also true. What else? Read the account in Mark 3:1-6 (or in Matthew 12 or Luke 6) and let me know what you think. Are we actually to be like Jesus when he exposed the unacceptable view of the religious leaders?

Fifty-one
Should Jews pay taxes?

During the final days of Jesus' ministry here on earth, opposition against him grew increasingly. Pharisees joined with their adversaries the Herodians to set a trap (*pagideuo* is a hunting term meaning "to snare or trap") that would give them grounds to turn him over to the Roman overlords. So, on one occasion they met him and, after flattering him with words about his integrity and willingness to speak his mind in any situation, they posed their cagey question about paying taxes to Caesar or not. A No answer would put him in trouble with the civil authorities and a Yes answer would cost him his popularity with the people.

At this point Jesus could have gone off on a long and complicated discussion of the role of personal religious choice in a complicated civil setting. Instead, he rather abruptly identified them for what they were, "hypocrites," and asked for the coin required for the tax. "Whose image is this on the coin?" he asked, and they said, "Caesar's." And now comes his response: "Give to Caesar what belongs to him, and to God what belongs to him." The authorities, taken aback at his answer, fell silent, and slipped away.

That is how Jesus handled the situation. Rather

than allowing his opposition to trap him into solving the dilemma with words, he took action and that put them on the defense. A masterful stroke. So now comes the question for today's believer who wants to imitate Christ in his daily conduct. Is there anything here that is transferable to us today?

Several things come to mind. First, he clearly identified his opposition. They were "hypocrites," feigning an interest in the question of whether the Jews should pay taxes imposed by the Romans while the purpose of the entire charade was to trap Jesus. The Greek *hypokrites* is a "stage actor," pretending to be someone he is not. While it may not always be helpful to call opponents undesirable names, it is a good idea to know and name one's rival. Second, to make his point Jesus didn't rely solely on words. He simplified the issue by turning it into an interchange that actually involved their participation. Learning is more effective when it is objectified as much as possible. There on the coin was the carved image of the emperor. Seems obvious that the coin bearing his inscription should go to him. It belonged to him, but other things belonged to God. For us this suggests that we need to think through the issues and be able to make the most plausible argument to support them. And finally, he apparently did not boast about winning the argument. The authorities were set back with nothing to say and found a way to leave as quickly as possible. Jesus did not taunt them.

Fifty-two
The power of simplicity

In the last chapter we used the account of Jesus' encounter with the Pharisees to illustrate how Jesus handled himself in a situation in which he could have been trapped. I would now like to use the same encounter to demonstrate the way Jesus got to the heart of an issue by simplifying it.

When they asked him if it were proper for the Jews to pay the poll tax, he asked for a coin and requested them to answer whether or not it should go to the one whose image was on it. They were unable to answer because either a Yes or a No would leave them defenseless. Only one thing to do – don't speak.

So what did Jesus accomplish in this encounter? I believe he made his point by simplifying the issue. He could have gone into a long discussion about the relationship of religion and government, or addressed the ethical problem facing the Jewish people by virtue of the dilemma between their faith and their moral responsibility to Roman overlords. Instead, he said, "Give Caesar what belongs to him and to God what belongs to him." In clarifying the issue he used a principle quite similar to what is known as KISS, "Keep it simple stupid" (Note: no comma, as it was stated originally). Jesus took what could have become an exceedingly complicated issue and made it simple. Advance in every intellectual discipline is the triumph of simplicity over complexity.

Simplicity has become the goal in many areas of life. Japanese art forms, such as painting, theater, and flower arrangement, all reflect the beauty of simplicity. Karl Barth, the famous German theologian, summarized a lifetime of scholarly research with the words, "Jesus loves me this I know for the bible tells me so." John Calvin praised "lucid clarity" as the goal for writing. Take almost any sentence you have written and remove every word that isn't absolutely necessary and you will be surprised how much better it reads. Simplicity has a remarkable charm and strength.

So, as Jesus simplified the issue of where to give what, we would probably do well to remove from our lives the unnecessary clutter of stuff. Issues are complicated only when sufficient time hasn't been given to thinking them through. Lives become complicated with too many unclassified responsibilities. Jesus became incarnate to solve the complexity of mankind's moral history. He did it by dying and rising again.

Simple, clear, and powerful! Our Savior's life recommends that we adopt what might be called

Christian minimalism. When you get right down to it, some things are so vitally important that other things must be set aside. KISS.

Fifty-three
Clarity and Confidence

The story about giving Caesar what belongs to Caesar closes with, "taken back by Jesus' answer, they fell silent and slipped away" (Luke 20:26). On the same day Jesus answered another question, this one having to do with life after the resurrection, adding that the Sadducees "didn't have the courage to ask him anything else" (Luke 20:40). Then, after answering a question posed by the Pharisees, Jesus noted, "From that point on no one had the courage to ask him any more questions" (Mark 12:34). Finally, Jesus took a question asked by some Pharisees and turned it back on them; and, since no one was able to answer, "from that day on no one dared to question him further" (Matt. 22:46). These four consecutive encounters (and Jesus' response in each) yield an important insight as to how Jesus lived out his life: Fully informed, he spoke with clarity about every issue. So much so that his adversaries were left with open mouth and afraid to pursue the discussion.

If he did, the charge to live like Jesus would be preposterous. But he lived among us as one of us and we are to live as he did. What does that imply? Did this ability belong uniquely to Jesus alone or should it be characteristic of us as well? As you would know from my posts, I believe that the incarnate Jesus was fully human and did not live out his life by resorting to the use of his divine nature.

One thing is that he was fully informed. No one was able to ask him a question he couldn't answer. I believe that every follower of Christ should make scripture their fundamental book for life. We need to know how Yahweh dealt with his people prior to the coming of Christ. We need to be able to answer questions about how Jesus lived, what he taught, how he died for our sins, and how he will return. We ought to be able to turn immediately to relevant verses for answers to every basic problem of life. One result of a thorough knowledge of scripture is the ability to answer relevant questions with clarity and certainty. The believer should approach all of life in a way that mirrors his Master. Tough call? Yes, but we follow the example of one who was able to combine certainty with compassion.

Fifty-four

Jesus' Lament over Jerusalem

Jesus was a man of many moods. He is normally pictured in the gospels as patiently instructing his disciples or speaking to large crowds. I have to believe there were also times of good humor when, around an evening fire, he exchanged stories that brought a smile. At the same time, there was a somber side to his public ministry. Both Matthew and Luke report that moment when, looking out over the city, he cried out, "Oh Jerusalem, Jerusalem! How often I have longed to gather you in my arms as a hen gathers her chicks under her wings, but you wouldn't let me. Look, there is your temple, forsaken by God!" (Matt. 23:37-38)

In the heart of God there is a deep desire for the restoration of man. History took a tragic turn from what God had in mind, leaving an empty void in the heart of man. When Jesus reflects on what it is that has replaced what might have been, his heart is heavy with sorry. So on this day his mood was controlled by the sad realization that man had taken the wrong road and was now suffering the consequences of the choice.

I ask, what is the role of sorrow in the life of today's serious believer? I believe we can learn from

Jesus' experience that genuine sadness is the proper background for the coming joy of restoration. Sadness over the tragic results of sin is a proper part of the mindset of every mature Christian. In the Beatitudes, Jesus pronounces blessed "those who understand the sorrow of this world, for God himself will comfort and encourage them" (Matt. 5:4). Sadness and joy have a unique relationship. Each intensifies the other. Sadness is even deeper when one realizes the infinite delight of joy, and joy soars beyond expectations against the background of sadness. Each plays its rightful role in the life of the believer. The lost-ness of man apart from the saving process of grace brings an increased earnestness to the active believer and the joy of eternal friendship with the One who crafted us in his own image deepens the sadness we experience along the way. May we join Jesus as he looks out over our Jerusalem longing to gather the rebels back into the safety and provision of God.

Fifty-five
What's going on around you?

One day during his final week in Jerusalem, Jesus sat down near the temple in the Court of the Women to watch as people dropped money into the treasury chest. That Jesus paid attention to what was going on around him was intentional. The rich came by and with a flourish deposited their coins. Then a poor widow approached and quietly dropped in two little copper coins (worth about a penny). Jesus called his disciples over and made the point that the widow had given more than all the others because, unlike those who gave what they could spare, she gave what she needed to live on (Mark 12:41-44 and parallel in Luke 21).

Obviously, there is the lesson that a gift is valued not by its monetary worth, but by what it "costs" the giver, but what strikes me is the attention that Jesus gave to the activity itself. He was interested in what people were doing. If we had been there, we would have noticed a certain amount of pride in how the affluent carried out their giving and, by way of contrast, would watch the poor widow as she quietly slipped the two little coins into the box. Jesus was aware of all that was going on and he wanted his disciples to be sensitive to that simple incident that demonstrated such an important point. Great lessons are often mirrored in minor acts.

What can we learn from this? One thing is that to live like Jesus calls on us to be sensitive to all that is going on around us. Life is not a solitary journey, but a communal experience. It can be as rich as we choose to make it by cultivating a conscious awareness of those who travel with us. Fixation on one's self narrows the experience. It rules out that fullness that comes when others play a significant role in the adventure. But more importantly, a strong sense of what is going on in the lives of others alerts us to needs that we may be able to take care of. Life is as rewarding as we allow it to be by maintaining a constant awareness of others who travel the same road. Jesus chose to fix his attention on others, not on himself.

There is a story about a man who always played nothing but one note on his violin. When asked about that rather strange custom, he said, "I've found my note, others are still looking." The application is that by concentrating on how Jesus lived (rather than on what he taught) we seem always to end up noticing his concern for others. That was his "note" and the more we hear it, the more important it becomes. It seems true that Christ-like living is, in a rather broad sense, giving attention to how we can help others in their journey through life.

Fifty-six

Should charlatans be exposed?

In this column we have watched how Jesus lived rather than what he taught. We've been trying to clarify what it means to live as Christ did. In the course of writing I have come to see that included in this category are those insights that come from his demeanor under various situations as well as perspectives he held on different issues. They are not a part of what we would normally refer to as his teaching, but they certainly provide an example for us to emulate. Today's piece is one.

Jesus, along with Peter, James, John and Andrew, had gone up the Mount of Olives and, looking back, they saw the beautiful temple. This prompted them to ask him when all the things he had promised would happen. Jesus warned them about charlatans who would come, claiming to be the Christ. They would insist that the end is already here. "But before the end," said Jesus "there will be war, earthquakes and terrible signs in the sky" (Matt. 23:3-8 and parallels in Mark 13 and Luke 28). What Jesus "did" was to inform the disciples of the danger of false teachers.

Many of the problems of that sort in today's

church existed in the early days of Christianity. For example, Arianism got its start (and name) with Arius, an Egyptian priest who lived and taught in Alexandria in the third century AD. It taught that Jesus was not the eternal Son, but was created by the Father and therefore not divine. That doctrine is still alive in the more liberal wing of Protestant Christianity.

If Jesus were with us today, I believe, from his response to the disciples regarding end times (see above), that he would "warn us about charlatans (i.e., liberal preachers and teachers) who would lead us astray" (Luke 21:8). Should we not do the same? One of the difficulties in being a biblical Christian is to unashamedly proclaim as true all that Jesus said was true. He warned his followers against those who perverted the truth, usually for some sort of personal benefit. Divisive? Yes, in a certain way. But truth needs to be set free from all its perverted forms. Error is always a twisting of the truth.

So the fact that Jesus warned his disciples about those who would come with a message that was not quite true, our responsibility is to know what is true and to be willing to die for it if necessary. That's exactly what happened to Jesus on the cross!

Fifty-seven

To Warn or Not to Warn?

One day several disciples went to Jesus to ask about the time of destruction that was to come on Jerusalem and its temple. Jesus warned them to be on the lookout for charlatans who would try to lead them astray by claiming that the time had already come and that they were the promised Messiah. The disciples were not to be fooled because, before that would happen, there would be an extremely difficult time of international war, famine, earthquakes, and terrible signs that filled the sky. Jesus warned his disciples about the spiritual damage that could come from those so-called prophetic voices that claimed knowledge of the future. He was concerned that the believers to whom he was writing be led astray by false teaching.

So, how can the fact that Jesus' warned his disciples be applied to the life of a believer today? Are we responsible in some way for what might be called the purity of the faith? One example might be the recent decision in our nation's capital to declare the legality of same sex marriage. Some would consider that a legal, not a moral, concern and therefore not relevant. But aren't laws a reflection of what a people hold to be right or wrong? If so, then the issue becomes ethical, not merely legal. For example, speed limits are not arbitrary decisions, but exist because we hold the moral principle that human life ought not be endangered by fast moving cars. It seems logical that, if we believe that marriage is intended by God for one man and one woman, we should let our voices be heard against any change in the divine plan. Jesus warned about false teaching, so should we not correct heresy whenever it arises?

I get the feeling that we tend to handle Christian heresies by pretending they don't exist. "Get along, go along" is the mantra we constantly hear. Since the context in which Jesus spoke had to do with events yet future, should we not allow the amillennialist to believe one thing and the premillennialist something else? Jesus warned against charlatans who distort truth, so shouldn't we do the same? But, you say, which position is right? I believe responsible Christian scholarship should go to work and solve such issues. The time is over for scholars to start with the conclusion and then expend all their energy on proving it in a scholarly way.

Fifty-eight
How Jesus prevented "burn- out."

During the final period of his ministry, Jesus spent each day preaching in the outer court of the temple. It was there that he continued to teach "the people," the *laos*, (not the *ochloi*, the crowds). However, each evening he would leave the city and spend the night on the Mount of Olives, probably in the village of Bethany with his friends Mary, Martha, and Lazarus. Since the religious authorities were watching him closely, looking for some excuse to arrest him, his departure each evening was probably due to the need for the quiet atmosphere of a friendly home. In any case, each morning he would return to the city and people would flock to hear him teach.

That he left the city each evening suggests that he needed regular breaks in order to restore both body and inner self. Teaching such important issues to such large groups – from dawn to dusk and in the open air – had to be emotionally draining. Jesus took those quiet hours to allow his Father to restore and redirect his energies. We know from the recent Olympics that you can't run a 10 K meter race as if it were a sprint. Energy must be carefully allocated so it isn't missing in the final lap when it's so crucial. We've all heard of ministerial "burn-out." My feeling is that rather than a sign of success it may well be an indication of failure, the failure to schedule times for renewal. It seems clear that God wouldn't assign spiritual responsibilities impossible to carry out. Could the zeal we often display in trying to do the job better than its ever been done, be an expression of pride? I tend to believe that "burn- out" in the world of pastoral ministry is an indication not of achievement but of failure. Every evening Jesus left the place of activity and went "home" to be with friends and his Father. Should that not be our model?

It is hard to admit that spiritual progress is something that we as mortals cannot achieve. But the natural cannot perform supernaturally and spiritual progress is not something that we as mortals can do. Our sole responsibility is to open ourselves so that he can work through us. God's power "is made perfect in [our] weakness" (2 Cor. 12:9). So, like Jesus, we need regular periods of refreshment. No one but you can make that decision in your life.

Fifty-nine

How skilled are we at "foot-washing?"

The Passover meal had been prepared and Jesus was in the upper room with his disciples. Just prior to the meal Jesus got up from the table, removed his robe, took a basin of water and began to wash his disciples' feet. He explained that what he was doing was what they should do for one another. It was by taking the role of a servant that they would enjoy the blessing of God (John 13:1-20).

By this one act (recorded only in John) Jesus established forever the basic principle of Christian conduct, that is, serve the other. Contrary to our nature as fallen human beings, we are to take the role of servant in all our relations with one another. That's it! Were we to carry out this one fundamental principle, everything would be changed dramatically. Imagine a local congregation where each member adopted as their basic rule for living, the simple question, "How may I be of help to you?"

Impossible, you say. Probably, but isn't that the nature of ethical norms? I remember doing an article on the Sermon on the Mount for ISBE and learning the various ways that Christian thinkers have tried to explain the unattainable level of conduct it requires.

One answer is that it isn't relevant to our current situation because it was intended for the "Kingdom age." Another is that the high ethical standards intend to make us feel guilty, so that in desperation we will turn to God pleading his mercy. My conclusion was that "impossible goals" were not meant to discourage us, but to continually hold before us the perfect example as a continuing guide for living.

What would it be like to always take the servant's role? In almost every situation in life there is the opportunity of serving the other. The servant steps aside when he and someone else arrive simultaneously at the same door. The servant with more than he needs responds to the one in need. The servant puts the best interpretation on a story that could make the other look bad. The servant husband begins his day asking how he can make his wife's day more enjoyable. I doubt if there is a single bit of time in the day when it isn't possible to serve someone else. Even if a person is alone on a desert island, it is always possible to pray.

So, as Jesus arose from the table and took the lowly task of a servant, you and I can get up from our comfortable seat of self-centeredness and find some "feet" that need washing.

Sixty

Was her anointing a waste?

One of the more poignant moments in the life of Jesus was that day in Bethany when a woman came into the house where he was having dinner with friends and anointed his head and feet with expensive perfume. You'll remember that his disciples were offended by what they considered a wasteful use of precious ointment. They offered the crass suggestion that it would've been better to sell it and give the money to the poor. I am quite sure that Jesus looked them straight in the eye as he asked, "Why are you criticizing this woman for such a beautiful expression of devotion?" (Matt. 26:10). Then he explained to them that by her anointing him with ointment she had prepared him for burial. What she had done was so significant that it would be told as a memorial to her wherever the message of his death and resurrection was proclaimed.

What exactly was it that was so memorable in her action? It's true that the perfume was worth a year's wages, but Jesus saw something more important. Was it not the deeper significance of her devotion? As he shared with her the experience, he was moved by the sincerity and affection of the noble act. The disciples saw nothing but a meaningless waste of valuable oil. Judas, the traitor, thought he had a better idea: Sell it!

What a different response by Jesus! Here was a woman with the quiet audacity to enter uninvited into a house where others were dining and to anoint their guest with precious ointment. Jesus understood the depth of love that moved her to take this unusual step. He shared with her the importance of the moment. While others saw the act, Jesus grasped what it meant to her and was one with her in that holy moment.

The significance of Jesus' response on this occasion is important for those who want to live as Christ did. It is quite clear that it calls us to look beyond whatever the act itself might be. Those who live on the surface enjoy their non-involvement because it provides them time to pursue their own interests. Jesus was constantly considering what was happening in the life of the other. Her devotion touched him at a profound level. He valued her by identifying what she had just done as "a beautiful expression of devotion."

The model for us is clear. Things are not what they may appear to be on the surface. It is beneath the surface that we find reality. A flower on her birthday is, well, far more than a flower; it is an expression of love. Acts reveal what is going on, but what they mean must be discovered on a deeper level. Like Jesus, may we pay less attention to what others may do or say and focus more on what their word or act reveals.

Sixty-one

How to handle active threats

As Jesus was sharing the Passover meal with his disciples he became profoundly disturbed in spirit. He let it be known that one of them would betray him. The disciples were stunned by his words and in their confusion looked around at one another asking, "Lord, It couldn't be me, could it?" Jesus said that he would dip a piece of bread in the sauce and give it to one of them. That would be the one who would betray him. Jesus held the bread before Judas and in a tone I suspect was both gentle and firm, told him to go ahead with what he intended to do. I can imagine a long pause before Judas accepted the bread and then, quickly leaving the room, went out into the dark night (Mark 14:18-21 and parallels).

It was certainly with great personal anguish that Jesus watched one of his own disciples turn against him. They had all been so close for three years. Jesus did not berate him or accuse him for the coming act of betrayal. Very quietly, but very directly, he answered Judas' "Is it I?" with "It is just as you have said." By his gentle manner, Jesus was making it easier for Judas to change his mind and not follow through with his act of betrayal. When that did not happen, he had no option but to let the truth be known. Jesus had done everything he could to prevent Judas from carrying out a plan devised by Satan.

To display such a remarkable quality of character in the contemporary world is not easy. When faced by someone who intends to harm us, the natural response is to take the initiative and harm them first. The way Jesus reacted would have been better. We could have waited in quietness as the act began to unfold, praying that God would bring to our assailant's mind the sinfulness of what he intended to do. Strength of character is not measured by how vociferously we defend our reputation. If we are living in love – and we must be if we are living a Christ-like life – we will relate to those who would harm us exactly as Jesus did that night in the upper room.

But, you say, that's beyond our ability. And you are right. Scripture has never counseled us to live the spiritual life in our own power. There is an immeasurable difference between the two levels. The good news is that God has supplied us with the power to live as Christ did. The Holy Spirit dwells within and is fully capable of providing the strength to meet every challenge.

Sixty-two

What's the best part of every day?

After the Farewell Discourse (John 14:17), the group in the upper room sang the Passover hymn and Jesus went out "as was his custom" to the Mount of Olives (Luke 22:39). The phrase in the Greek text refers to "an usual or customary manner of behavior, a habit" (BDAG). That it is included, indicates that on this occasion Jesus did what he always did, that is, he moved from the center of attention to a place where he could gather his thoughts and open his heart in prayer. His disciples followed him, but Peter's strident defense of his live-or-die commitment to Jesus was certainly out of place as they walked to Gethsemane.

What I want to stress is that times for serious reflection were a customary part of Jesus' life. He went to the Mount of Olives because it was customary (not necessarily the place but the purpose for going). We know that customs are helpful or not depending on what the custom is. On this occasion Jesus left the upper room to meet with his Father. It was what he did on a regular basis. For us to reflect Christ in our lives we should have that same habitual practice. Ideally that custom should simply reflect what we do, but what if it doesn't?

It seems clear that if our lives don't have the custom of regular times alone with the Father the next best thing would be to develop the habit. So how do we go about that? The most important ingredient in developing the habit is a genuine desire to become all that God desires for us. It requires a lot of "want to." Lackadaisical commitment leaves us at ground zero. There will be no habitual practice apart from an ardent desire to make it a reality. The upside of this is that as the custom develops, it becomes easier to maintain. Soon a day will seem strange if that encounter has not happened. We recognize the importance of relationship on a human basis. I'm not sure whether or not "absence makes the heart grow fonder," but I do know that life deprived of significant relationships is a miserable way to live. And for the Christian, a life lived where contact with one's heavenly companion is sporadic is not the joyful experience it was meant to be. The old adage of "being too worldly to enjoy God and too spiritual to enjoy the world" is all too true in many lives.

My suggestion is to have regular time alone with God. Whether it is on our knees in a quiet place or out for a walk in the park doesn't matter. What does, is that the practice of enjoying the day with our Father be a vital part of everyday.

Sixty-three

The calm after the storm

The account of Jesus and his crucial prayer in Gethsemane is for me the most deeply moving episode in the life of Christ. It was there, after pleading with the Father to take away the cup of suffering, that he yielded to his destiny as the Sacrificial Lamb, saying, "May it be your will that is done, not mine" (Mark 14:36 and parallels). This final commitment followed a time of "deep distress" that rolled over him like a great wave, and "fervent prayer" that caused his sweat to fall to the ground like heavy drops of blood. To exacerbate the incredibly difficult situation, when he returned to where his disciples were stationed he found them sleeping. This happened three times. Against this background we see Jesus admonishing them rather gently while supplying as an excuse for their failure to stay awake, "Man's spirit is willing, but human nature is weak." After the last return, he added, in what appears to be a rather normal tone, "Rouse yourselves! Let's be going. Look, here comes my betrayer" (Matt. 26:46).

What captures my attention in the story is that after such a crucial time of testing (no one will ever fathom the depths of Jesus' commitment that led him to bear our sins) Jesus displays an emotional composure that is calm and remarkably balanced. Subsequent events relate how he discussed with those who came to arrest him their reason for picking that particular place and moment, how he healed the servant's ear that had been slashed by Peter's impulsive sword, and how he turned himself over to the authorities as his disciples fled. He was in complete control. His final acceptance of the Father's will seemed to grant him complete composure for the events that were about to happen.

Obviously, you and I will never have an experience like that, but it is true that once our faith has turned into conviction, a great calmness will cover our days as well. Instead of worried adjustments for every minor issue of daily life we will be able to accept whatever the day holds with a serenity somewhat like that which we see in the Gethsemane encounter. If God is in control of our life, what happens will be part of that plan and his plans for each of us are the best of all possibilities. There is no need to be anxious because we are no longer responsible for what happens, only for how we react to them. Living like that reflects the way Jesus lived.

Sixty-four

The composure of commitment

The armed guards arrived in Gethsemane, Judas delivered the traitor's kiss, and Jesus freely identified himself as the one they were looking for. This was too much for Peter, so he drew his sword and slashed off the right ear of the servant of the high priest. "Put your sword back where it belongs," Jesus instructed. Then he touched the wound and the ear was restored. Calmly he asked the guards why they hadn't come for him during the day when he was preaching in the temple – and the disciples fled in terror.

What strikes me is the remarkable composure of the man who just a few hours before was in deep anguish as he committed himself to the Father's will of death on a cross. The disciples fled for their life, one of them stark naked, having lost his robe in the struggle. What is there here that can help us live in a way that will reflect Christ, especially in terms of the aftermath of a difficult emotional ordeal? In this series on learning from what Jesus did (as over against what he taught) we have taken the position that Jesus lived his incarnate life as one of us, as a fully human person.

That means that he did not draw on his divinity to

perform miracles but relied solely on the power of the Holy Spirit. In Gethsemane he had just made his ultimate commitment to the Father's plan. Now he is calm and handles the immediate concerns as though they were normal affairs. How did he manage that?

It seems that the secret of his composure was the completeness of his commitment. Had he come from the garden with any uncertainty it would not have been possible. So we learn from him the importance of a complete acceptance of God's will for our life no matter what. Our decision made; we will carry out exactly what God wants, no exceptions. This provides a wonderful sereneness that allows us to do in a calm and confident manner whatever is the next thing. For Jesus it was going through the incredibly dark experience of Calvary, for us, the next difficult trial.

Sixty-five
The beauty of a quiet spirit

The temple guards had put Jesus under arrest and taken him to the house of the high priest. When questioned about his teaching, he reminded Annas that his teaching had always been done in the open, so why was he being questioned; they already knew what he taught. At that a guard slapped Jesus in the face, asking how he dared speak like that to the high priest. Very calmly Jesus asked for evidence that his teaching was not true, and added, "If not, why did you strike me?" (John 18:23). Jesus was then taken to Caiaphas where the high priest and all his cohorts kept trying to trap him into saying something they could use to condemn him. To all their accusations Jesus simply "said nothing" (Matt. 26:73). He did not defend himself.

Once again we see the serenity with which Jesus responded to his accusers. To Annas he provided a simple answer; to Caiaphas and the clerics who had gathered (unlawfully, since it was night) he remained silent. He did not defend himself. In Jesus' reaction to all of this we see two remarkable characteristics: composure under stress and the willingness not to defend oneself. Both of these run counter to human nature. In times of distress it is especially difficult to maintain the emotional balance that keeps us from doing or saying the wrong thing. When accused, especially if the accusation is false, we rush to our own defense. It is what we do because of who we are. We are made that way. But apparently Jesus had no desire to prove himself before others, especially the ruling class, which at that time was the religious leadership. I have a feeling that, in most cases, one's reputation is enhanced by saying nothing. At least it deprives others of the pleasure of displaying their superiority by countering what you said.

It seems to me that both of these qualities are extremely important in the life of the believer. They display a high level of spiritual maturity. It may not be our lot to face false arrest with the potential of death, but we do face difficult situations with significant consequences. Certainly a steady hand and a careful tongue will serve not only our own personal interests, but the reputation of God as one in whom we may trust. If God is in charge – and we believe he is – then there is nothing in our life in which he is not in some way involved. A personal set back, say . . . sickness or financial loss, need not disturb our trust in him since he is the One who is always there to help. He didn't cause it, but he can and will, if we let Him, use it for our ultimate benefit.

May God grant to each of us the serenity of genuine faith, and may our days be spent with a calmness that overcomes the inborn desire to defend oneself.

Sixty-six
How to handle betrayal

Annas had failed in his attempt to successfully question Jesus, so the guards took the accused to the house of Caiaphas the high priest. Peter followed along at some distance, but when he arrived he joined the guards around the fire. At one point, a maid of the high priest asked Peter if he were not one of the Jesus group. Peter denied it, and when he was asked for the third time, he swore by God that he did not know the man. Just then, as Jesus was being taken through the courtyard, a rooster crowed. Jesus turned and looked Peter "straight in the eye." Suddenly Peter remembered the words of Jesus that before the cock would crow that very night he would have denied him three times. To have Jesus look so directly into his eyes and realize that his master was fully aware of what he had done, was simply too much for the Galilean fisherman. He went out and "wept bitterly" (Luke 22:60-61).

What I would like to know is what happened in that moment. What was Jesus "saying" by his direct look into Peter's eyes? What passed through Peter's mind just then? What we do know, is that Peter broke into tears. The sudden awareness of having denied the

One who so recently he had declared to be the very Son of God, was more than he could handle. For Peter it was an encounter with reality. He, a believer, had betrayed the One in whom he claimed to believe. How could that be? How corrupt is the human heart?

I think several things happened when Jesus looked Peter "straight in the eye." One is that he wanted Peter to realize that he knew about his failure to remain true under trial. The failure was not something that could be swept under the rug as though it never happened. Sin needs to be clearly labeled as sin. You have to get it out to get over it. However, it was not a look of condemnation. It had never been a policy of Jesus to use shame as a way of achieving his goal. Peter was guilty, that was true, but Jesus wanted him to know that he was not abandoned. The bonds of genuine friendship are not so easily broken. Jesus wanted Peter to understand that while his denial was wrong, restoration was his for the asking.

How does this event inform us as we consider our desire to reflect Christ in our life? The two things that stand out to me are first, the willingness not to retaliate, and second, the desire to restore broken relationships. The two are inseparably joined: Satisfy self (retaliate) and you can't achieve the other (restoration). Should we not let the other know by our look that their offence against us, although wrong, cannot break the relationship?

Sixty-seven

When is it best not to answer?

When Jesus was being questioned before Pilate he responded to the four different questions they asked, but when they began to level accusations against him he "made no response, not even to a single charge" (Matt. 27:14). He answered questions about whether or not he was the king of the Jews, but he didn't respond to empty allegations. What does this suggest as to what we should do when we find ourselves being questioned about our faith?

It is important to note that when he answered their valid questions, he did so in a polite and effective way. When asked if he were the king of the Jews he responded, "The words are yours" (Mark 15:2). When Pilate thought he had caught him implying kingship, Jesus said, "You are the one calling me a king" (John 18:37). But when valid questioning gave way to false accusations Jesus simply did not answer. It is commonly known that an effective gambit in "discussion" (read "argument") is to put the other person on the defensive.

Suddenly their explanation of why they did or said something turns into a defense against things they didn't do or say. It seems to work every time and Jesus understood the evil intention of his accusers. He did not respond to a single one of their phony claims against him.

The lesson for us in this story is to not be tricked into defending ourselves when accused falsely about some aspect of our faith. An example might be the claim that we think we are going to heaven because we are such good people. A wrong response would be to list all the good things we have done in life, as if the number of our good deeds had placed us on the fast track to heaven. Not only would we have been tricked into supporting a false doctrine, but would have wasted time and energy in doing what worked against us. Silence is the answer to questions like that. At the same time, when given the chance to explain our faith to a nonbeliever, we should answer with wisdom and grace. That is what Jesus did. It is a helpful idea to think of him when facing the moral and religious questions of life. "What would Jesus do?" is still the best question to pose to one's self in all those critical moments.

Sixty-eight

When saying nothing is best

When you read the story of the trial of Jesus before Pilate, (it takes you all the way from that point in time to a cross on Calvary's hill) you will be struck by the fact that Jesus is recorded as speaking only once. Let's watch what goes on during this tragic period.

When Pilate heard the crowds identify Jesus as a Galilean, he breathed a sigh of relief and sent him to Herod the Tetrarch who was in charge of that area. Jesus refused to perform a miracle for the Roman tyrant, so he was returned to Pilate who declared him innocent. But to satisfy the crowd, Pilate said he would have him whipped and then released. That didn't satisfy the crowd so Pilate gave them a choice between Jesus and a guilty rebel by the name of Barabbas. As to Jesus they keep shouting, "Crucify him!" Jesus said nothing.

At that point Pilate had Jesus turned over to Roman troops who stripped him of his clothing and put a scarlet robe on him. Twisting thorny branches into a crown, they jammed it down on his head. Then kneeling at his feet, they mocked him as king, spit on him, and beat him severely with his staff. Jesus said nothing. When returned to Pilate with crown and scarlet robe, the crowds shouted, "Crucify him! Crucify him!" Jesus said nothing.

Once again Pilate took Jesus inside and in all seriousness asked him where he came from. When Jesus refused to answer, Pilate reminded him that he had authority to set him free or to crucify him. It was at that point that the record says that Jesus spoke. He told Pilate that his authority as a Roman governor to make the decision had been given to him by God. And that is the only recorded utterance of Jesus during this sequence of actions. Unable to withstand the demands of the mob, Jesus was flogged and Pilate had him released to the soldiers for crucifixion.

The dignity of our Lord in this appalling series of cruel and debasing events is remarkable, beyond belief. Falsely accused, he said nothing. Unjustly beaten, he said nothing. Publically humiliated, he said nothing. What does that say about how we are to live as Christ lived? The answer is clear: When unfairly accused, remain silent. If you didn't do what they said you did, any attempt to exonerate yourself is useless. Truth is enhanced by the quiet refusal to explain why we didn't do what we didn't do.

Sixty-nine

The benefits of forgiveness

When Jesus arrived at the place of execution, the Roman soldiers offered him some wine mixed with a drug called Myrrh. He took a sip, but found it too bitter to drink. Then they placed him on a wooden cross, nailed his hands and feet to it and raised it upright. Hung between heaven and earth, the Son of God gave his life as a ransom for our sin. I believe he was looking down on the battle-hardened soldiers who were dividing up his clothing when he prayed, "Father, forgive them, they don't know what they are doing." What a remarkable act of forgiving love!

Forgiveness is the decision not to repay, the willingness not to seek revenge. Some might regard it as an indication of weakness, but Gandhi was correct when he said, "Forgiveness is an attribute of the strong." That Jesus – in pain from the scourging, the long trek to Calvary, being nailed to the cross – was able to muster the strength to pray that God would forgive his tormenters, is beyond comprehension. Apart from supernatural strengthening, to undergo such an ordeal would have been impossible.

It is obvious that to live as Christ lived we must be

willing to forgive those who have belligerently blocked our path in some way. That there can be no exceptions is clear from the fact that Jesus forgave in the most radical situation – he forgave his executioners. He even acted like a defense lawyer and stated the grounds on which the guards could be forgiven. Earlier he had taught his followers that being forgiven depends on one's willingness to forgive. The critical words are, "If you do not forgive others their sins, your Father will not forgive your sins" (Matt. 6:14-15).

Forgiveness is a power that changes the life of the forgiver. It frees the one who embraces it and puts it into practice. No longer do they have to be concerned about paying back the offender. Revenge demands that we give full attention to getting even and that concern robs us of our only irreplaceable treasure – time. And while we are spending precious time trying to figure how to get even, our supposed offender goes scot-free. That's a bad tradeoff! Sin has a way of destroying the one who sins. In a similar way, forgiveness blesses the one who forgives. Once we get our minds off ourselves, it is easy to see that actions, good or bad, undoubtedly benefit or harm the doer more than the recipient. Who can deny the pleasure of those given to random acts of kindness! While forgiveness is specific rather than random, it certainly brightens the day of both.

Seventy

Can empathy be learned?

The crucifixion was over and the crowds had begun to dissipate. Standing somewhat at a distance were the women who had followed Jesus from Galilee to be of help (Mark 15:40). Among them was Mary, the mother of Jesus. It probably comes as no surprise that standing there beside his mother was John, the "beloved disciple." Although Jesus was in intense pain, his thoughts went out immediately to his mother, grieving as only a mother could in that situation. Looking with love at his mother, Jesus, said, "Mother dear, John is now your son!" Then turning to John, he added, "My mother Mary is now your mother!" (John 19:26-27) We are not sure about his father Joseph, but it is assumed that he had passed on. Scripture says nothing about his siblings at this point. So Mary in her sorrow and loneliness needed care and John, such a dear friend, was exactly the right person.

How can we live in such a way as to reflect that kind of personal concern for those we love? Empathy is defined as the "vicarious experiencing of the feelings, thoughts, or attitudes of another." It is reaching out with the heart to touch another. And Jesus was that kind of man. Obviously, empathy is a quality of character expected of those who profess to have surrendered themselves to Him. To care deeply for another may be easier for those born with that temperament, but there is no excuse for "empathy deficit" (as Kirsten Powers put it) in the life of the believer.

Note, as well, that Jesus' feelings of deep concern for his grieving mother did not stop at the point of being empathetic. It moved him to take the necessary action. I would think that it was not accidental that John was standing there by Mary. From what we know in scripture of the disciples, John would be the one to be there in a place to help. Perhaps this shows something else about the empathetic Christian – they seem always to be in places where need may arise. I have the feeling that for most, life is so busy just staying alive that little time is left for dealing with the needs of others.

May God grant us the willingness to learn from his Son how to become the kind of person who is sensitive to the deep need of others and moved to do something about it.

Seventy-one

"Mary!"

It was early Sunday morning and two of the women close to Jesus and his disciples had come to the tomb to prepare his body. Upon arriving, they saw the stone rolled away and an angel of the Lord in dazzling white met them with the glad news that Christ was risen. The two women were told to go and tell Peter and the others that Christ was risen from the dead. Mary the mother of James left, but Mary Magdalene remained behind in tears. As she sat facing the empty tomb she heard a voice behind her. Believing it to be the gardener, she asked where the body was so she could go and get him. His response was a tender and loving, "Mary." Turning she cried out in wonder and joy, "Rabbouni!" We understand that she probably took ahold of his feet because he said to her, "You don't need to hold on to me; I'll be here for a while before I go to my Father." Never has there been a more moving reunion than this. All Jesus said was, "Mary!" and in that moment her affection for her "Teacher" could not be restrained.

It has always been intriguing to me that the first person to see the resurrected Jesus was a woman from whom seven demons had been expelled (Luke 8:2). In view of the importance of Peter in early Christianity, one might assume that he would have been the first to whom the resurrected Jesus would have appeared.

But he heard about it from the women and even then, he and the other disciples questioned the report. So Peter and John went back out to the tomb to see whether or not it was merely an idle tale. I'm inclined to believe that Mary was the first to see Jesus because her love for him was the greatest. Not that love can be quantified, but it just seems so appropriate.

What does that encounter say to us in terms of how we should live? It's simple; we should love like Mary. Taking "seven" as symbolic we can say that Mary's love was perfect and complete. It lacked nothing. In life there are varying degrees of affection. Mary's put her before the tomb, weeping for the loss of her Teacher. What do you suppose the rest were doing? Perhaps they were at the local "pub" coming to grips with the very real possibility that their hopes for prominence in the coming kingdom may have been misguided? That Peter and John had to run out to the empty tomb to verify a woman's report suggests that they had already considered returning to fishing.

What a moment! What a remarkable love by a woman from whom seven demons had been cast.

Seventy-two

Scripture and the burning heart

It was Sunday afternoon and two of Jesus' followers were returning from Jerusalem to the town of Emmaus. As they were walking along the way, Jesus joined them and asked what they were discussing. They marveled that this man would ask, because everybody knew about the Galilean preacher by the name of Jesus who had come back from the dead that very morning. That remarkable event was all they could talk about. When the two men told Jesus all about it, he chided them for not knowing that Moses and the prophets had taught that the Messiah would suffer. Then he pointed out all the passages in scripture that spoke of him. When they reached their destination, Jesus was going to continue, but at their invitation he stayed for the evening meal. It was when he took the bread and broke it that they realized who he was. At that point Jesus disappeared from their sight. Cleopas and his companion looked at each other in astonishment and said, "Did not our hearts burn within us as he spoke to us along the road, explaining scripture?" (Luke 24:32)

This encounter is one of the most endearing passages in the gospels. The two men were simply returning from the capital city filled with wonder at what everyone was saying had happened. They were intrigued by the explanation of the one who had joined them. However, it was at the table, when Jesus broke the bread that they suddenly caught on who he was. And then he was gone. They looked at one another and confessed that they should have known because while he was explaining scripture along the road – "Did not our hearts burn within us?"

To realize the deeper meaning of scripture is to experience the "burning heart." Truth needs very little support from logic. We have all felt the warmth of divine truth when we have learned it along the road of life. Even the more secular world acknowledges the "ring of truth." And this truth warms because it puts us in a vital relationship with God, the One who is speaking through it. It's important to realize that scripture is not simply words in a book. The purpose of scripture is to allow you to fellowship with and learn from God. It is when a favorite passage becomes God himself speaking as being there that the heart begins to burn. The Fourth Gospel tells us, "The Word became flesh and dwelt among us." He did, and when his presence is revealed to us, I can guarantee that our hearts will begin to burn. May our life be a Walk to Emmaus along with Jesus.

Seventy-three

The sudden appearance of Jesus

Jesus had risen from the dead, Mary had seen him, the disciples had been told that the tomb was empty and Peter and John had run there to see if the report were true. But now the disciples are huddled behind locked doors for fear of the Jewish authorities. Then the seemingly impossible happens: "Suddenly Jesus appeared right there in their midst" (Luke 24:36). Thinking it was a ghost, they were terrified, so Jesus chided them a bit asking them to take hold of his hands or feet to make sure he was real. He explained that everything that was happening to him had been written in the law and prophets. Then he did something of crucial importance – "He opened their minds so they could understand the Scriptures" (Luke 24:45).

There are two points in this story that are especially relevant to how we are to live in our relationship with Jesus. The first is that He has a way of suddenly appearing in our midst. Is it not true that Jesus was actually there before he "suddenly appeared?" We know that at the moment of faith God is said to dwell in us. So if he is "in us" is he not always "with us?" We know from Hebrews 1:15 that God has promised never to leave us nor forsake us. So we can say that although Jesus "suddenly appeared" to the disciples, it doesn't mean that he wasn't with them prior to that moment. He didn't come through the door, because he was already there. The point for us is that we are to be aware of the constant presence of the resurrected One. He is always with us for guidance, strength, encouragement, and for sharing the joys as well as the trials of daily life. That he may not be physically materialized has nothing to do with the reality of his presence. Remember, "I will never leave you nor forsake you!"

The other point is related: For us to understand scripture, we must allow him to open our eyes. The gospel account is not a series of words organized to convey something. Of course, there are words, and they say something, but words, like Jesus, have a way of "materializing" when our eyes are opened. They communicate. God wants to actually speak through the words of the biblical authors, but for that to happen we must by faith have the veil removed. Then we can hear him say, "I love you and have forgiven you in Christ." In the life of every believer there are those faith-filled moments when the words of scripture become the actual voice of God. And that is the way to read scripture. Let God speak.

Jesus suddenly appeared to the disciples (although he was always there) and He suddenly speaks to our heart (although we tend to be too busy for extended conversations). To be mentored by Jesus is to recognize his presence and listen to what he wants our heart to hear.

Made in the USA
Coppell, TX
10 February 2023

12439868R00105